Aging Comes of Age

Aging Comes of Age

Older People Finding Themselves

Frank Hutchison

Westminster/John Knox Press
Louisville, Kentucky

© 1991 Frank Hutchison

All rights reserved—no part of this book may be reproduced in any form without permission in writing from the publisher, except by a reviewer who wishes to quote brief passages in connection with a review in magazine or newspaper.

Scripture quotations from the Revised Standard Version of the Bible are copyrighted 1946, 1952, © 1971, 1973 by the Division of Christian Education of the National Council of the Churches of Christ in the U.S.A. and are used by permission.

Excerpts in chapter 6 from *Sex After 60* by Robert Butler and Myrna I. Lewis are copyright © 1976 by Robert N. Butler, M.D. Reprinted by permission of Harper & Row, Publishers, Inc.

Excerpt from "God's World" by Edna St. Vincent Millay. From COLLECTED POEMS, Harper & Row. Copyright 1917, 1945 by Edna St. Vincent Millay. Reprinted by permission of Elizabeth Barnett, Literary Executor.

Book design by Ken Taylor

First edition

Published by Westminster/John Knox Press
Louisville, Kentucky

PRINTED IN THE UNITED STATES OF AMERICA
9 8 7 6 5 4 3 2

Library of Congress Cataloging-in-Publication Data

Hutchison, Frank, 1909–
  Aging comes of age : older people finding themselves / Frank Hutchison. — 1st ed.
     p.   cm.
  Includes bibliographical references.
  ISBN 0-664-25188-9

  1. Aged—United States—Psychology. 2. Self-actualization (Psychology)   I. Title.
HQ1064.U5H87 1991
305.26′0973—dc20   90-46779

Dedication

This book is dedicated to my wife, Doris, who encouraged me to consider that working on this book was more important than anything else I could do with my present life. With patience and insight she listened as each chapter in early draft form was read to her.

Congratulations to my contemporaries, who are living on a level never attained by previous older generations and who are now setting a standard of excellence for those who will follow them.

Thanks also to dear old friends such as Franz Schubert, Wolfgang Amadeus Mozart, Franz Joseph Haydn, Robert Schumann, George Gershwin, Frédéric Chopin, Felix Mendelssohn, Ludwig van Beethoven, Edward McDowell, Sergei Prokofiev, Antonin Dvorak, Aaron Copland, and Sergei Rachmaninov, whose inspiring music sustained me during the long hours of writing this book.

Contents

Introduction		1
1.	Welcome to a Wider World	5
2.	Explore Your Inner Self	11
3.	Never Give In—Never, Never, Never	17
4.	Be Proud of Your Age	25
5.	Sustain Your Sense of Belonging	33
6.	Sex, Sexuality, Sensuality, Love	39
7.	Expand Your Spiritual Well-being	47
8.	Stretch Your Mind to the Limit	57
9.	Seek to Broaden Your World	69
10.	Experience the Rich Life of a Volunteer	77
11.	Be Out of Step as Much as Possible	85
12.	Be Ever the Advocate	93
Epilogue: Make Your Life a Work of Art		101
Notes		107

Introduction

We are beginning to take what one day will be recognized as a significant step in human development. Older people of today are making a sharp break with past aging theory and practice. We are exploring ways to continue to contribute to society and to have a satisfying personal life in the years ahead.

Older generations have undergone unprecedented changes in recent decades. Millions of men and women of retirement age are enjoying a richer, more satisfying life, one of greater fulfillment, than ever before. Fifty years ago there was Grandma Moses, who made news when she started painting in her late seventies. Today we would not consider such activity exceptional.

For the first time in history older people are asking a basic question: What shall I do with the rest of my life? No matter our previous experience, the issue is what we make of ourselves from today on. Will we waste the years ahead, tossing them aside in trivial pursuits? Or will we look upon the future as a rare treasure, a time to bring out the very best in ourselves?

In the 1970s and 1980s, the aging patterns characteristic of the past began to shift. Not only did people live longer, they also moved out in new directions. They started new businesses following retirement; they returned to colleges and universities for degrees or for further professional training; they became world travelers. They entered the arts, took on full-time volunteer jobs, and set new patterns of divorce and remarriage. Not only did they live longer (the fastest growing age group today is eighty-five and older) but they achieved a kind of renaissance.

In 1932 Walter Pitkin's best-seller, *Life Begins at Forty*, affirmed that one's middle and later years could be productive and enjoyable. His title reflected the changes that had been experienced by that time. People were no longer worn out at forty; they were able to enjoy life for years after that. Now, almost six decades later, longevity and increased life purpose have reached still higher levels. We can say that for millions of Americans a fuller life begins at sixty.

The full extent of today's gerontological revolution is not clear at present. We can only guess as to how many of the more than 30 million people sixty years of age and older have been emancipated from ageist thinking and outmoded patterns of life. Ten million? Fifteen million? We do know that as of 1990 the American Association of Retired Persons (AARP) had 33 million members aged fifty and older. Moreover, today's burgeoning older generation will seem almost insignificant when all those born during the baby boom after World War II begin to retire.

Shortly after the year 2000 those born in 1946 will become fifty-five years of age, and over the following two decades there will be 75 million people added to the senior group. They will probably be the most enterprising retirement generation ever, for they have been holding down two or three jobs and involved in every kind of enterprise. The earlier youth culture and the various life-styles will be adapted to new circumstances. Women will become a more powerful force in society because of their employment experience and the family responsibilities many of them have borne as caregivers of older parents or as single mothers supporting their households.

Even as these baby boomers look toward retirement, many of them will be kept in the work force because of the declining number of younger persons to take their places. After the turn of the century the nation's work force will inevitably include many of the older generation, whose skills and experience will be sought by business and industry. Every kind of inducement will be offered to them to stay in the business or professional world or to return to it.[1]

Perhaps the new generation of older men and women are like the flowering of spring after a long winter. Could their life in the past be likened to a form of hibernation? Are they Rip Van Winkles, emerging from a long sleep to find themselves living in a world unlike the one they knew earlier?

Life-style changes for older people are so new that even the latest books on aging say little or nothing about them. A recent 600-page textbook on gerontology has only a few sentences suggesting that some of us are emerging into a wider world. Nor do historians of aging deal with the phenomenon. For example, in his excellent volume *How Old Are You?*, dealing with America's changing age consciousness, Howard P. Chudacoff does not refer to any significant differences in aging patterns today other than the increase in longevity of the older generation and the marked increase in its numbers.[2] Historians tend to avoid considering anything still in the developing stage. They prefer to quantify and categorize.

This book is not so much *about* older people as it is an attempt to talk with them. It seeks to inspire older people to see the expanded years ahead as far more productive, satisfying, and enjoyable than ever before—if they seriously wish them to be. This is more a "why to" book than a "how to" book; actually, it is an "ought to" book.

Aging Comes of Age seeks to publicize this unparalleled development in our day and to illustrate it in some detail. It is designed for a new breed of people of mature years who are beginning to realize that their potential, when fully actualized, can bring them lives of greater satisfaction and accomplishment. Through their emerging maturity they are demonstrating that they are unique, the first second-chance generation in history, something new under the sun.

This positive view of today's older people does not overlook the cold fact of death. It comes to all of us one day.

Nor does it deny the hard realities of disease, frailty, and helplessness that cruelly afflict many elderly. Of the more than 30 million people sixty years of age and over, perhaps as many as 7 million suffer various disabilities.[3] One cannot say enough in recognition of these older persons who live in pain, at risk, or at death's door. Nor can we do enough to alleviate their sad lot. Yet they make up no more than one fourth or one fifth of the older segment of the population.

There is, however, far too little recognition and acclaim given the substantial majority. At least 23 million older people are free from crippling ailments, senility, terminal illness, and other disabilities that would hinder their involvement in the normal world. These 23 million have the promise of a life of substance and satisfaction far exceeding anything known by previous generations. This book seeks to do justice to this important major group.

Aging Comes of Age covers the broad range of life that can be enjoyed by these persons. It challenges ageist thinking, opposing all instances of submission to stereotyped life patterns. It outlines the mature life at its best. It shows the vital importance of high self-esteem and urges the exploration of the self to find inner fulfillment and self-actualization. It accepts and encourages sexuality in later years and urges a quest for sustaining spiritual values. It views enlarging one's mind as an absolute priority, suggesting three areas of significant further study. It emphasizes the vital importance of being a serious volunteer and highlights the need for advocates and activists in today's society. The book also points out why older people should be unconventional in thought, word, and deed. In short, the book directs men and women toward the meaningful years following retirement, which in our day can be as much as one third of our entire lives.

1
Welcome to a Wider World

From the age of classical Greece, philosophers have spoken of the unplumbed depths of human nature. In our own day, too, religious teachers and psychologists assert that our powers are boundless.

Erich Fromm, the German psychotherapist, has said that we

> possess not only the ability to speak and think but also the capacity for ever deeper insight, greater maturity, a capacity for love and for artistic expression. All these things are potentially present in us, waiting to be developed. Activity . . . means just that: the bringing out, the manufacturing of those powers that human beings have but usually remain hidden or repressed.[1]

We have the potential to explore life to the limit. However, the promise of a deeper and more complete life is seldom addressed to anyone past the biblical "three score years and ten"—or even to those in their sixties. A rare exception is found in the writings of Simone de Beauvoir, the French existentialist philosopher. In her *Coming of Age* she asserted that

> the greatest good fortune, even greater than health, for the old person is to have [the] world still inhabited by projects: then, busy and useful, he [or she] escapes both from boredom and from decay. . . . There is only one solution if old age is not to be a parody of our former life, and that is to go on pursuing ends that give our existence a meaning—devotion to individuals, to groups or to causes, social, political, intellectual or creative work. In spite of the moralist's opinion to the contrary, in old age we should wish still to have the passions strong enough to prevent us from turning in upon ourselves.[2]

There is a growing recognition today that life can have meaning and purpose for people in their later years. A wider world is opening up for those who were once considered permanently locked into a narrow existence.

It was discoverers like Columbus and Balboa and Cabot who opened new worlds to those living in Europe. In our day, older people are becoming joint discoverers. Men and women are embarking on a journey of exploration of life after retirement. They are pioneers in a new world where life at its best is not over when one's job ends or when the children leave home.

The title of the James Bond movie *You Only Live Twice* helps suggest that we can have one life before age sixty and another afterward. Older men and women are looking into the possibility that with open minds, expectancy, imagination, and lifelong experience they can create satisfying and productive later years. They are out to conquer new worlds!

A large number of men and women of postretirement age are already embarked on this journey. The movement will become a groundswell of enormous proportions in a few decades. When the 75 million people born between 1946 and 1964 start reaching retirement age,[3] they will move out into fresh creative experiences, following the lead of those of us who have already done so. Here are just a few examples.

Gene had been an insurance broker in Oregon, far too busy even to think of volunteering. When he moved to a Texas city upon retirement, his life changed radically. He helped set up a city-wide survey to identify which physicians and medical institutions would accept fee assignment under Medicare. The results were published with great acclaim in the local press. This was only the beginning. Now a full-time volunteer, he serves on the boards of eight community agencies. His life has taken on many new dimensions.

A learner all her life, taking courses when she could, Joan is returning to the university for a degree. Because she was married to an American soldier, she had lived with him and their children in Texas, Japan, and Germany. One son became fluent in Japanese and another in German; all five children are involved in their own careers. Now retired from a post in a senior center, Joan is set to complete her education. She knows it is never too late to go to school.

Another late achiever is a Canadian in his middle eighties who winters in Arizona. When I last saw Pete, he was planning a round-the-world trip with his wife and intended to write a book about how people in their later years could still become global travelers.

In Florida, Grace leads a group of other older women actively working to improve the homes of elderly low-income people. These women, not professional builders or even do-it-yourselfers in earlier years, now do carpentry and plumbing, and even tackle tough roofing jobs. With a few financial grants and considerable scrounging of aid from local builders, they have improved many dwellings.

Joanna realized that, in her southern city, an underprivileged area with many older people of varied racial groups needed an activities center. She imagined what she would wish to have available if she were an elderly low-income person. Although she had no professional experience in the field, she started a program to meet those needs, then looked around for support. Out of her concern came a community service benefiting thousands.

A woman eighty-six years of age agreed to assist a man who, though a high school graduate, was functionally illiterate. To help him get a promised building superintendent's job, Lucy spent many hours each week helping with his reading and writing. At the same time that she was engaged in this volunteer enterprise, she took swimming lessons, the first in her life. She told a reporter she had had two knee joints replaced recently, and, since the doctor guaranteed them for twenty years, "I expect to be swimming when I am 106."

A long-retired clergyman learned that his city was setting up a task force on the homeless and offered his services to the mayor. For more than half a year he devoted fifteen hours a week to attending meetings, interviewing homeless people, and preparing drafts for the final report. Meanwhile he continued to be a regular member of a local service club. At year's end the club gave him their Man of the Year award for his volunteer service, even though all the other members were younger than his daughters.

An old friend went to New York from California after his retirement as a college teacher of religion. He had decided to complete his doctor of philosophy degree at a theological seminary. His wife, Mary, for decades a language teacher, began working in the seminary's alumni office. Within a year she had mastered the computer and tracked down the whereabouts of hundreds of former students. Her husband was busy stretching himself in his old area of competence, but she had taken off in a new field of achievement.

Another husband-and-wife team, Pat and Mike, came to a small city following his retirement from the military. Mike was soon giving swimming lessons to children and older people. He actively promoted Senior Olympics, and both Pat and Mike won ribbons in swimming and field events. She has been active locally and nationally in a movement that seeks to change American research and industry from a military-oriented economy to one that benefits the whole of society. Each year they invite a foreign student to live with them.

These ventures have not moved the world appreciably closer either to utopia or the kingdom of God. However, these kinds of older-life activity, when multiplied millions of times, do result in social benefits that would not otherwise be experienced. As chapter 10 records, the contributions of older men and women volunteers have changed the face of modern society.

Even more important in both social and spiritual terms is what has taken place in the minds and hearts of these people. The same thing is happening with millions of others whose creative life experiences we can only imagine. Not only do they provide valuable services unavailable decades ago, they also enjoy a wholesome sense of continued vitality and usefulness. They belong to a group unique to America. They have joined ranks with all those mature men and women who have glimpsed a far greater life ahead of them and claimed citizenship in that wider world.

2

Explore Your Inner Self

Our lives today have been enriched by the contributions to self-understanding made by a man whose name may not be familiar to many of us. Abraham Maslow was born in a Brooklyn slum in 1908. Early in life he became fascinated by books, the wide world of the library, and the expanding life of the mind. He studied psychology and soon found himself caught up in a Freudian interpretation of life.

Eventually he asked himself, Why concentrate on neurotic, pathological, repressed, emotionally crippled people? Why not pay closer attention to all those men and women with great visions and expanded lives whose mere existence has enriched human life? Maslow examined some outstanding people he knew personally and then went on to look into the lives of other exceptionally healthy and well-balanced persons, among them Eleanor Roosevelt, Thomas Jefferson, Abraham Lincoln, Albert Einstein, Baruch Spinoza, and Albert Schweitzer.[1]

Maslow's great passion was to explore "the farther reaches of human nature." His concern was to have human beings experience their full potential, to have all persons become everything they are capable of becoming. His goal was to help create self-actualized persons: "What a man can be, he must be."[2]

The psychological and spiritual forces Maslow set in motion have touched us, whether or not we realize it. The awareness that there is a larger and deeper life potential has seeped into our consciousness. We have begun to realize that, if we genuinely wish it, we can enjoy richer and more significant personal lives.

We rarely ever come close to living up to the overall potential with which we are blessed. We may never have been challenged sufficiently, or we may never have fully realized what powers and inner resources we received as a birthright. Perhaps some summary descriptions of characteristics Dr. Maslow discerned in the people he studied over the years will expand our horizons and stimulate our imagination.

There is nothing beyond our understanding in these major findings concerning self-realization. All the qualities set forth strike a familiar and responsive note. In these descriptions you will see what you are—or partly so—and you may see what you could be. You may be able to picture yourself here and there—or at least a shadowy portrait of yourself.

Maslow learned that fully realized, self-actualized persons evaluate people and events by the facts at hand, not on the basis of wishful thinking, anxiety, or fear. They distinguish the fresh and concrete from the abstract and general. They perceive what actually and factually exists, rather than allowing their wishes, hopes, and fears to create a false world. They don't fool themselves. They are not threatened by the unknown. They are comfortable with it, often challenged by it.

These people accept themselves, others, and their world just as they are. They take the weaknesses and frailties of human nature, including their own, in the same spirit that they accept the various characteristics of nature—sun, winter, storms, earthquakes. They look upon the world with the wide eyes of a child—seeing, noting, drinking it in. Self-actualized men and women see human nature as it is, not as they wish it were. The only feelings of guilt these people are likely to have are generated when they recognize their own shortcomings.

With their ability to be spontaneous in almost everything, they are fully open to new experiences. Both in outward behavior and in the inner life of the mind there is a kind of youthfulness in their naturalness and simplicity. At times they may appear outwardly conventional, but this is simply to get along with society around them on trivial matters. Never does social pressure prevent them from doing what they consider right; they are truly ethical people. They are always themselves, always inner-directed. Because they are less inhibited, they are able to take risks, to stick their necks out on important matters. Life is its own reward, and thus they care little about honors, prizes, and prestige.

Self-actualized people are problem solvers, focusing on the problems, not on the needs of their own egos. Being inwardly secure, they are not concerned about themselves. They usually have a mission in life, a cause, a challenge outside themselves. It is not necessarily something they chose, for in a certain sense it chose them. Their lives are channeled toward purposeful goals.

Self-actualized people are industrious and work hard, but for them work is simply part of the joy and meaning of life. The usual sharp distinction between work and play is blurred. Work becomes play.

These men and women cherish privacy. They practice detachment. Fulfilled persons are usually in the public eye, yet they seek to retain an area of personal privacy. Because they are committed to an existence that is rich and full, they seek detachment from many of the surface distractions and activities accepted as normal by others. They usually have a conventional existence on the outside. Their difference from the ordinary person is within.

These fortunate persons have a freshness of appreciation. They enjoy with unusual zest all that makes up life—children, sunsets, a flower in full bloom, classical music. For them every new day is a revelation. No matter how boring much of normal existence may be to others, these folk find delight in everything around them. Life is an exciting adventure, one they prize and in which they delight. They enjoy all of life, while most people enjoy only the occasional moment, the peak experience.

They experience the mystical, they see beyond the seeable. They are often overwhelmed with a feeling that takes them beyond the usual five senses. An unaccustomed sense of awe and wonder may sweep over them. They often have feelings of unlimited horizons opening up to their vision. They live in two worlds.

These people enjoy deeper relationships than most. They have deep-rooted interpersonal dealings. They show more outward love and affection, are more in touch with other people, are more forgetful of themselves than others would consider possible. Usually tolerant about the shortcomings and mistakes of others, they are quite intolerant about cruelty, injustice, dishonesty, and hypocrisy.

Self-actualized men and women display a built-in, genuine, humble, democratic spirit. Although these people are blessed with both natural and acquired gifts, they still have a solid personal and egalitarian relationship with their fellow human beings. They are on a friendly basis with people everywhere, no matter what their politics, nationality, class, education, race, or color. They enjoy people.

They take seriously the issues of virtue and morality. One mark of fully realized persons is their clear distinction between right and wrong. Their morality is quite different from the average person's conventional morality. These gifted souls stand strongly for what historically has been right and moral, rather than giving in to expediency or contemporary pressures that lead some people to compromise basic principles. The ends and goals they seek are noble, beneficial to everyone, and promise long-term consequences for good. They believe in a meaningful universe, and therefore everything they do must fit into a larger purpose. They have a mission in life.

Such people enjoy a healthy sense of humor. Their wit is philosophical rather than destructively personal. It comments on the human condition, not on the peculiarities or weaknesses of others. They are able to see the funny side of many circumstances. They can laugh at themselves.

These people possess a sense of discovery and inventiveness that touches everything about them. This resembles the naïve creativity of unspoiled children, the fresh quality of life inherited by everyone at birth. "Most people lose this as they become acculturated, but some individuals seem either to retain this fresh and naïve way of looking at life, or else, if they have lost it, as most people do, *to recover it later in life*" (my emphasis).[3]

What all these persons have in common is a fresh approach to life, the expression of a healthy and human existence. A distinctive sense of originality and creativity is seen in everything they touch, in their whole attitude toward life. They are open and receptive to everything new.

Merely reading about these ideal character traits does not automatically transfer them to us. We must recognize that these qualities are available and can be shared by us all. But to realize they are available is not to say that these qualities are ordinary. We sense immediately how essential they are to attaining our highest achievement and fulfillment.

We need not possess a streak of genius to live more like fully mature beings. We older people can adopt most of these attitudes by self-examination and a change of perspective. We do not need coercion or pressure to move our lives to a higher elevation. All that is essential is a vision of what we can yet become, a hint as to what direction we might move, a road sign pointing the way.

You can use this description of what self-fulfilled persons are like and how they react to life's experiences as a checklist. Remember: there is no need to lament that you do not have all these virtues. No one does. The point is to be thankful for what you actually have and to pursue what might still be possible in your life. Having done that, recognize what you have achieved and enjoy yourself. Your future years will be rich and full depending on how well you realize your total potentialities, not on how you dwell on what you don't have! This is certainly an instance where, in the words of the old song, it pays to "accentuate the positive."

Remember, the fulfilled, healthy persons whom Abraham Maslow studied were not persons to whom something extra had been added. They were normal persons who capitalized on their full potential.[4]

All the qualities of life, all the attributes of totally realized persons, are available to us in our later years. Recognition of this potential can be the beginning of a new life for us.

Actually, Maslow did not discuss older persons and their possibilities as such. The particular characteristics of people advanced in years were not a subject of study in the 1950s and 1960s, when he was writing. But today we can accept his insights about the expansion of all human life, as he saw it, and then take one step farther in this new day.

The overall message should be clear: we older men and women are not locked in to what we once were. A new kind of future is ours to possess. All we need to do is develop our inborn potential.

We might well think of ourselves as the modern equivalent of last century's homesteaders, who went into the western territories as they were opened to settlement. These pioneers moved into a world new to them by staking out a sizable claim and then actually living out their future in that place. Today, all of us in our later years can stake out our own claim as to where and how we will live out our future. This life-important choice is up to us.

3

Never Give In—Never, Never, Never

In the 1940s, in England's darkest hour, Winston Churchill's courage and determination inspired the nation to endure the Nazi blitz by looking to the day when victory would come. His words, "Never give in—never, never, never," touched Britain's nerve and strengthened her people's resolve.

We older Americans who would see a bright new future ahead of us can take Churchill's words to heart. Many of us face challenges of illness, aches and pains, and, sometimes, exhaustion. We feel lonely. We miss the status our work once gave us. Friends and family change. We suffer staggering disappointments. We discover that nothing gets easier as we grow older. Infirmities of the flesh—and the joints!—make efforts to fulfill our chosen purposes more trying. The normal reaction is to relax, to let go, to take things easy. But, of course, to do so gets us nowhere in our quest for the larger life we have glimpsed so tantalizingly. The lesson is clear: never give in, never give up—never, never, never!

In our later years we are apt to forget the struggles we went through earlier in life. Could we ever have made the track team or the basketball varsity without strenuous effort? Didn't we work hard to get top grades in school and win a promotion on our first job? All mothers remember the experience of childbirth, an obvious example of how life demands unusual effort and often pain if anything worthwhile is to come into existence. Not all of us face Churchill's challenge of "blood, toil, tears, and sweat," but no step forward and upward has ever been automatic and without struggle.

What counts is the way we look upon our infirmity. If it arouses self-pity on our part, we carry around far too heavy a load. We should consider what happens as a challenge, a hurdle we have to surmount. Robert F. Murphy displayed this attitude when he was paralyzed by a tumor on his spine. As he described in *The Body Silent,* he came to reexamine the word "disabled":

> I was badly damaged, yet just as alive as ever, and I had to make the best of it with my remaining capabilities. It then occurred to me that this is the universal human condition. We all have to muddle through life with our limitations, and while I had certain physical handicaps, I retained many strengths. My brain was the only part of the central cortex that still worked well, but that also is where I made my living. *Disability* is an amorphous and relativistic term. Some people are unable to do what I do because they lack the mental equipment, and in this sense, they are disabled and I am not. Everybody is disabled in one way or another.[1]

All older people are handicapped in some way. Even our advanced years, by themselves, are a serious liability in today's youth-oriented society.

To be born with serious handicaps is to face difficulties throughout life. Our society now recognizes that children with handicaps of one kind or another have a right to special care, attention, and education. For the luckiest of these children, ingenious equipment is available, as are sympathy and understanding and classes directed to the child's particular needs. These exceptional children may develop into involved and contributing grown-ups.

For persons who develop crippling ailments late in life there is often neither understanding nor compensating equipment and training. Under the best of circumstances, seniors suffering from arthritis and other debilitating diseases seldom have little but pain-reducing medication to help them. Too often they have to grin and bear it, altering their habits and life-styles as best they can.

In such circumstances, possession of a larger vision can be determinative. Not everything can be overcome with willpower or even a sure sense of where one wishes to go. However, even with the physical and other difficulties that come with a long life, one can enjoy a more nearly normal life. A glimpse of what the years ahead can yet become can be motivating and inspiring. In some ways a handicapped person possessing a challenging vision is better off than a healthy person of comparable age who lacks a sense of what can yet be accomplished. Determination to overcome one's current difficulties often leads an older person to further achievements, no matter how cruelly he or she is afflicted.

In a recent biography of Isak Dinesen, of *Out of Africa* fame, the story is told of a champion French horseman. When asked how it was possible to get his horse over the high barriers in a steeplechase, he answered that he had to *"jeter le coeur"*: that is, throw his heart over the fence first.[2] Then it was easy to get the horse to follow. If, with our burden of many years, we first throw our hearts over the age barrier, the rest of us, body and mind, will follow.

There are many ways "to strive, to seek, to find, and not to yield," to quote Alfred, Lord Tennyson. Even people without crippling ailments find that life makes strenuous demands on them. So it was when the struggle against segregation was reaching its peak. Thousands of black people of all ages engaged in a protest march of fifty miles from Selma to Montgomery, Alabama. An older woman, Mother Pollard, said proudly after the five-day, fifty-mile march, "My feets is tired, but my soul is rested." She had the proper sense of values.

For older men and women a sustaining sense of values also includes self-esteem and self-confidence. It is not enough to "never give in." We also need positive values and drives to survive and thrive as older persons. An example is the way someone changed the romantic words of Elizabeth Barrett

Browning, "How do I love thee? Let me count the ways," to read, "How do I love me? Let me count the ways."

This encourages us seniors to have a high opinion of ourselves. The issue here is self-esteem, not brooding conceit, not the narcissistic expression of the early 1920s popular song, "I love me, I love me, I'm wild about myself." Rather, self-respect is our goal, an appreciation of ourselves, a recognition of what is good about us, now and in the years ahead.

It is an old but time-tested saying that if we do not love ourselves we cannot love others. If we have a negative outlook on life and a narrow view of ourselves, it is unlikely that we will have a high opinion of others. Jesus put the situation plainly: "Love your neighbor as yourself." This clearly implies that a modest self-love is essential to having a loving attitude toward our neighbors and, of course, toward life itself. Not to love is to be a zombie!

Some men and women, retiring from a lifetime of work, are often influenced by our work-oriented culture's view that the unproductive citizen does not count for much. The same inadequacy may be felt by parents when their children are grown and they themselves no longer can produce offspring—they may come to believe that they are no longer important.

A bit of questioning and soul-searching could help these men and women: "Wasn't I successful at what life required of me? Didn't I carry my own weight? Didn't I fill a niche God and society assigned me?" To see one's self as having fulfilled life's demands is to have a sense of having paid one's way over the years, of having been a winner in the game of life.

From self-esteem comes a feeling of self-confidence. What do the opera star, the Olympic athlete, the champion golfer, and the talented public speaker have in common? Self-confidence! They know what they are, they know what they can do, they are sure of themselves. Thus they do their own thing with ease, grace, and skill. We older people who have confidence in ourselves can achieve far beyond our fondest expectations.

So much depends on how we think of ourselves. A few years ago I dug out an old photo to send to my theological graduate school for use at my fiftieth anniversary reunion. I could hardly believe how youthful I looked at age twenty-five. I recalled what a professional handicap it had been to appear so young and immature. In those early years I felt that my youthful appearance gave me less authority with other people. I lacked confidence in my years, training, and experience.

In recent years, the opposite has happened. I benefit now from having thought of myself as too young, much of my life; I still have a youthful image of myself. In this way I can avoid much of the diminishing feeling some people my age have. What was once a psychological handicap has become a benefit. The image I once had of my youthfulness has simply carried over to my advanced age.

How we older people perceive ourselves affects not only how we appreciate ourselves but also whether or not we function as fully mature individuals, whose lives are still of value. What is important are not our outer wrinkles but rather the inner wrinkles of experience and insight that are embedded in our brains and our consciousness.

Some of us have problems of sight or hearing, of diminished strength and mobility, or other handicaps that make life a problem at times. We have to remember that much of our lives have been given over to conquering handicaps of one kind or another. Think how difficult it was not to know how to ride a two-wheel bicycle, connect with a baseball, or skate! None of us was born with these skills. And how frustrating it was in first grade to stumble through our reading!

Now that we approach the other end of the lifelong learning process, we still have to master new skills, new ways of doing things, in order to keep abreast of an ever-changing world. You and I must be open and honest with ourselves about this. Seriously, is it not a welcome challenge to have to cope with new demands? When we overcome this or that problem brought on by our advancing years, do we not feel the same as we did when we hit our first home run or won a school prize? The same self-confidence can be ours, if we are still willing to work at it.

What we say to ourselves largely determines what place we will take in the totality of things. How do we fit into the wide sweep of life?

Walt Whitman had something to say about that. It is not likely that more than a century ago the great poet was thinking of people of our advanced age. (Life expectancy then was only forty years.) But what he wrote touches us as though he had us oldsters in mind:

> The sum of all known value and respect
>   I add up in you whoever you are;
> The President is up there in the White House
>   for you. . . .
>   It is not you who are here for him . . .
> All doctrines, all politics and civilization
>   exurge from you . . .
> All architecture is what you do to it
>   when you look upon it . . .
> All music is what awakens from you when you are
>   reminded by the instruments . . .
> Happiness is not in another place,
>   but this place . . not for
>   another hour, but this hour . . .

Whitman declares that our legitimate pride in ourselves and our outreach to all of life give us a touch of the divine. This sense of divinity can continue to grow in our experience.

Finally, Whitman asserts, happiness and knowledge are not for some other existence: "Not in another place, but in this place—not for another hour, but for this hour."[3]

These are words we older people can thrive on. We are important. Our lives count. Everything God and humankind have created is to bless us and enlarge us. You and I are the end of everything—and also the beginning.

An appreciative look at ourselves can result in self-esteem. From this can come a genuine confidence in ourselves, the conviction that we can still successfully undertake new enterprises. This self-perception will help us see that in the years and decades ahead of us we can accomplish almost anything we set our hearts on. The outcome is self-empowerment—the power to fight against ageism and discrimination, the power to tackle tough jobs, the power to continue being the mature and productive persons you and I were meant to be.

Never give in to despair or to a feeling of approaching death. Rather, surrender yourself positively to all the impulses that urge you to believe that the years ahead of you will prove to be the most meaningful time of your entire life.

No one else is going to pursue the new vision for you. You are not alone in your search, for others like you are engaged in similar pursuits. But, in the last instance, your fate is entirely in your own hands. You are the one who has to assert for yourself that you will never cease pursuing your dream, will never surrender to accepted conventions and popular "wisdom," will never give in.

4
Be Proud of Your Age

Anyone who intends to move out in fresh creative directions will encounter ageism in various forms. Friends who were content with you as you were may look askance if you take on a new life-style character. People with more traditional views of aging will say that you are too old to change: "You can't teach an old dog new tricks." Still others may even break their relationship with you because you are no longer the "same person" and they no longer feel comfortable with you.

How will you respond? Will you extinguish the new light that glows within you, relinquishing the larger view you now have of the years ahead of you? Or will you ignore the criticism and follow your finest instincts? Many enterprising individuals in past generations, like Susan B. Anthony in her struggle to get the vote for women and Christopher Columbus in his search for a new route to India, have had to face similar opposition as they sought to take new steps.

In today's America you and I live in an environment that labels age unfairly. If a teenage boy forgets something important, it is because he is still learning. If a woman in her forties is forgetful, it is because she has so many things on her mind. But if an older person cannot remember something, no matter how trivial, obviously it is because of age. In today's world there are many double standards, and this is clearly one of them.

Three of the most significant areas of life in which older people often receive treatment quite different from that experienced by people half their age are in religious institutions, in the medical world, and in the employment field.

Religion. Our churches and synagogues have many dedicated ministers and rabbis, with a high concern for their ministry. They wish to render service and they call upon the power of God to bless and benefit those coming to them, whatever their age. Nevertheless, these clergypersons often lack gerontological training, insights, and awareness; they have not been schooled to recognize the peculiar spiritual, social, and other problems faced by people in their later years. A Facts on Aging quiz given to 140 clergy revealed that their level of knowledge of the aging process was no better than that of a group of undergraduates given the same test.[1]

Thus, when a man or woman of mature years comes for help because of marital difficulties, clashes with children, or other personal problems, the clergyperson is likely to put the client in a special category: This person is old and, being old, must feel anxiety about becoming infirm and facing death. Right away, a subconscious mental screen filters out what the older person is actually saying. And so the religious counselor may talk about putting one's trust in God, having faith in the hereafter, and so on. What was on the visitor's mind and heart gets bypassed. The older person receives a religious homily instead of a careful consideration of the problem and some suggestions about possible solutions.

In recent years a primary institution in the religious education field commissioned a nationwide survey of the relationship between religious faith and the development of one's life and thought. In many seminars across the country the Gallup study findings were rated by clergy, laity, and theological educators. I attended one such evaluation. There we learned that the survey had been carried out in terms of specific age groups.

The study noted the responses of people in four age brackets: 20, 30, and 40 years, and "50 years and above." At that point it was clear to me that the survey was invalid, at least as to what it concluded about the upper age categories, because people in the second half of life—60, 70, 80, 90, and older—were all grouped together. Ten years makes as much difference between persons of 50 and 60, or 60 and 70, or 70 and 80, and so on, as it does between persons of 30 and 40, or 40 and 50.

To me this was one more indication that even top religious bodies and their leaders are uninformed about today's aging. It was evident they did not understand that older people differ, one from another and from those younger. It is unlikely that older people will be served adequately by their local religious leaders as long as such ignorance of the gerontological aspects of their senior constituency persists.

Not all spiritual counselors fully realize that at age sixty a man or woman may have as much as another third of life ahead. We should expect this factor to be in the forefront of their thinking when counseling those of advanced years.

Medicine. Few older people are so fortunate as to have a physician as well trained to care for seniors as pediatricians are for children. A child specialist will prescribe only drugs suitable for children. He or she will not use medicines and dosages designed for adults, because children's bodies are quite different from those of grown-ups. Older people do not always have prescribed drugs suitable to their advanced years.

It is likely that young children receive more exact medical diagnoses than do most people age 60 and older. Many mental difficulties in older adults are misdiagnosed. For example, the effect of an overdose of drugs on older persons may wrongly be considered to be evidence of Alzheimer's disease. Similar erroneous diagnoses are made of frail elderly persons afflicted by acute malnutrition due to inadequate and unbalanced diets. Many older people suffer greatly, often fatally, through being given drugs suitable only for people half their age.

Almost worse than wrong diagnoses and prescriptions is the psychologically damaging treatment many older people receive from physicians who hold traditional views of the aged. Ken Dychtwald, a popular lecturer in the field of gerontology, has estimated that there are not more than one hundred fully trained geriatric physicians in this country.

Employment. In the employment field, also, ageism rears its ugly head. With federal laws prohibiting job discrimination on the basis of age, employers and personnel directors have come up with other excuses for not hiring people over fifty-five. For example, they tell older applicants that they are overqualified.

Older people not only do not get positions for which they are qualified, they are often shunted into low-paying temporary jobs. Employers too often assume that persons in their late fifties and early sixties have passed their prime working years. They also rationalize that older persons require less income than a younger man or woman. Years ago this discrimination may not have been as important a consideration. But now people are remaining healthy and living longer, and they are struggling with the reality of inflation. Thus, such employment policies hurt older people who seek employment both to retain their self-respect and to earn scarce retirement dollars.

How can you and I handle these forms of discrimination? Your first reaction should be to see them for what they are—bias, prejudice, stupidity. They say nothing about you as a person: your abilities, your real self. Hold your head a bit higher when discrimination touches you.

There is only one way to combat ageist discrimination: protest it whenever it appears and take legal action if warranted. Join national organizations that fight discrimination based on age. In the meantime, age bias remains a disturbing fact of life. Accept it as part of a less-than-perfect world the same way you accept the reality of a windy, rainy day when you planned a picnic or a day at the beach.

To offset possible age stereotyping by the leader of your church or synagogue, nothing is as effective as a face-to-face conversation. Politely raise the issue of discrimination based on age found almost everywhere. Ask about religious institutions. What about this particular religious body? Is his or her own ministry to older persons today different from a decade or two ago? Does she or he ever preach on today's unique older generation?

If this interview and later discussions do not satisfy you, perhaps another local religious body would provide a better answer to your needs. This issue is important because it touches sensitive aspects of your whole being.

As for the medical field, how does one locate physicians with competence, experience, and concern in geriatric medicine? If your community has a medical center, ask the director for suggestions. Your phone book might list a doctor with gerontological skills. Ask a specialist in Alzheimer's disease to recommend a general practitioner trained in geriatric medicine. The director of a senior center can probably recommend a physician who will fit your needs.

Finding the right physician is essential to your total well-being. You need a doctor who is as right for you as a good pediatrician was for your children. Protecting and preserving your health is worth all the time and effort you can put into the search for the right medical person. Your life could depend on this search.

When there is suspicion of possible ageist discrimination on the part of an employer or personnel director, raise this question, preferably with a witness present: Am I being judged by my record and documented skills or by my chronological age? If you are turned down for a position and you suspect discrimination based on your years, go to your state employment office and make an official complaint.

Demonstrate against age bias politely but firmly, standing for your rights in all situations. As a representative of a new breed of older person, it is up to you to show what today's people of advancing years are in terms of their self-regard and their grace under pressure.

This carries over to areas of personal handicaps such as

hearing difficulties and physical infirmities. Strangely enough, older people may discriminate against themselves. They can fall into the trap of believing about themselves what ageist scuttlebutt says about them. For example, they can be painfully self-conscious about wearing hearing aids.

Those of us who wear these helpful instruments obviously rejoice that they are available to us. We should wear them proudly, not apologize for them. They signify that we want to be fully aware of what is going on around us, fully involved in all of life. We wish to hear so that in turn we can speak and be heard by others. We are in the world today by virtue of our length of days, and we insist upon being involved in it as long as we live. How good it is that these new gadgets help both our hearing and our self-esteem!

Wearers of hearing aids not only hear what is going on around them, sounds they missed earlier, they may hear some things better than ever. For example, I played the violin when young, not knowing then that it was the wrong instrument for me. I had a deficiency in the upper range, so I should have tackled the cello or the bassoon. Miraculously, now that I have hearing aids designed to strengthen my upper register, I hear Isaac Stern's highest violin notes, which I once could only imagine in my mind. How wonderful at my age to hear something new. Many people do these days. C. Everett Koop, the recent Surgeon General of the United States, has said that he can now hear music that was entirely lost to him until he began to use hearing aids.

Another important consideration is that some older persons, thought to be senile, have been found to be merely hard of hearing. What seemed like mental confusion disappeared when they could hear again. At the other end of the age scale, some young children are often assumed to be mentally retarded, but when they are fitted with hearing aids, their personalities change as do their school grades.

So I proudly wear my hearing aids, as all my contemporaries should if they are needed.

Of similar importance is any device or piece of equipment giving mobility, convenience, and various forms of help to older persons with some form of disability. There are two considerations as to wheelchairs and similar helps. The first is obvious: they make possible much involvement in daily life that otherwise would be out of the question. A wheelchair, whether battery-driven or hand-powered, takes one around the home and out into the world. Without this mobility, the handicapped man or woman would be either room-bound or housebound. In either case, the individual would be deprived of "liberty and the pursuit of happiness," two of the three qualities endowed us by our Creator, according to the Declaration of Independence.

Of significance, also, is the state of mind of the person concerned. The pilot of a wheelchair, like the wearer of hearing aids, shows that he or she wishes to be fully a part of the active world, involved in all the interests and concerns of normal people. This use of willpower determines character. The harder one has to fight against isolation and immobility, the more the person's willpower affects all aspects of living and thinking. To conquer the wheelchair is to be more able to overcome other difficulties and barriers. Every victory over a disability makes one more alert, more flexible and adaptable, more equipped with a mind and heart ready to tackle anything that comes along. Would Franklin Delano Roosevelt have become president without his polio attack and the long fight he made to overcome its crippling effects? Some would say no.

Generations ago the blind were either street beggars—still true in many parts of the world—or housebound prisoners. Now with Seeing Eye dogs, long white canes, and instruction in becoming self-reliant, they become part of the outside world. What must be their self-esteem as they venture forth into a world which until recently was dominated by those with eyes!

For older people with visual impairment, one's attitude is

all-important. Activity, participation in life, and the employment of one's talents must continue despite this massive handicap.

Of course, with older folks, as with others considered disabled, nothing becomes easier with age. However, when disabilities are attacked forthrightly, there comes a driving force to help us overcome all that would hold us back. This is what fully self-actualized persons are discovering.

Someone has said that one's present age is exactly the right one. Would we wish to be Shakespeare's puking infant again, or a teenager wrestling with sexuality and a troubled self-image, or a thirty-year-old single parent with three small children and a full-time outside job? Over the years most of us developed the attitudes and feelings that have prepared us for whatever advanced age we happen to be. Accept your present age as the best age for you!

5

Sustain Your Sense of Belonging

All of us belong to someone or something. No normal person is so detached from life that he or she has no ties, no involvements, no connections. It is only the mentally impaired individuals who have no sense of belonging. They are lost in a vague wilderness, cut off from everyone and everything. They are strikingly different from most older men and women, who have a strong sense of belonging, which they cherish and seek to sustain and increase.

This sense of belonging to persons and causes distinguishes Dr. Maslow's fulfilled, mature men and women from ordinary people of whatever age. A useful exercise for those of us in our later years is to look back over our lives, reviewing the events and relationships of the decades gone by, to see what most touched and molded us. We can then determine—if we have not already done so years ago—to what we feel most akin, to what we belong.

In this search for the vital connections that have led to our expanded life and our sense of identity, we must begin with our own family. Even if we have expanded our spiritual and geographic horizons over the years, even if we have seen all people everywhere as part of our family, we have to start with our immediate circle and our extended family, living and dead. This is where I began some time back.

My paternal grandfather, James Hutchison, died during my infancy, but my father told me about him. A descendant of Scottish immigrants, he had serious books in his house and was a leader in his Presbyterian church. He worked as a carpenter-builder, when not planting his fields or caught up with harvest demands. When my father built our family house in 1904 he used the tools and aptitudes he had inherited from his father. As a young boy I played with his jack planes, chisels, and saws while making model boats, and today I still have a collection of those handmade tools.

I also still have books my paternal great-grandfather Philip read. Among them are Flavius Josephus' *Antiquities of the Jews* in an 1805 leather edition, collections of sermons, a 1680 edition of John Milton's poems, and, of course, a large eight-inch-thick 1816 family Bible, which lists the births, marriages, and deaths of half a dozen generations. It includes vital information concerning Cornelius Hutchison, who fought in the American Revolution. For some reason it does not mention my father's father as a member of the northern forces in the Civil War, but he was there at the battle of Antietam.

Through a kind of miracle, an edged-in-black six-page 1799 newspaper telling of the death of George Washington still survives in readable form. (Fifty years ago I put it behind glass, and today it hangs on my dining room wall.) This eastern Pennsylvania paper, the Reading *Weekly Advertiser*, printed a commemorative editorial: "Mourn, O Columbia! Thy Father and Protector is no more. Mourn, reader of whatever tongue or clime thou be, the friend of Liberty and of Man is gone." It described the funeral procession and gave excerpts from the Senate and House resolutions. What is especially fascinating about this paper is that, since it was published in late December of 1799, it was reputedly the only paper reporting Washington's death that month. That means it was the only one so reporting during that year of 1799 and therefore, with the turn of the century, the only newspaper to report Washington's death in the eighteenth century!

On our dining room wall is a framed print of George Washington, which years ago was taken from the first solid biography of the president, *The Life of George Washington*, by Supreme Court Chief Justice John Marshall. The book originally belonged to my great-grandfather Philip. Near the print of Washington is one of Abraham Lincoln taken from our family copy of the Nicolay and Hay biography of the assassinated leader. Apparently, my father's family was concerned about the man who was president at the time my grandfather fought in the war.

George Washington and Abraham Lincoln are still far-off historical figures to me, but I have the sense that these great men belong to me. The awareness that they were contemporaries to my family ties them to me.

I never knew my father's mother. The existence of my father, his two brothers, and two sisters is ample proof of her existence. In addition, on one of our walls hangs a hand-woven dark blue and white bedspread she made more than a hundred years ago. It has American eagles and plants in its design. All it lacks is her name woven into the edge of the material, as was often done in those days.

My other grandfather, Philip Schull, lived next door to us as far back as I can remember, until, following Grandma Mary Jane's death in 1920, he moved in with us. He was a part of our family until his departure from this life in the late 1930s at age eighty-nine.

This tall man, whose shock of white hair suggested photos of Mark Twain, was of fundamental importance in my life, and I cherish the thought that I belonged to him. He served as grandfather to all the children in our neighborhood, repairing broken toys and bikes and patching up bruises and wounds. His five-months-a-year schooling for five years—the only education available in his isolated Western Pennsylvania farming community in the 1850s—did not prevent him from being an avid reader. I recall seeing *Camille* by Alexandre Dumas and Mark Twain's *The Adventures of Huckleberry Finn* in his room. He devoured the Pittsburgh and Kittanning papers, always enraged over the current Republican president and his administration. "Those blackguards!" he would exclaim. "Those rattlesnakes! Those poltroons!" (He never used profanity; he did not need to!) His idol, whose large picture hung in his bedroom, was Woodrow Wilson.

In my youth there were no American Indians in or near our town, although it had been an important Indian camp and a prison for captured white settlers in the 1700s. In 1753–54, George Washington traveled up the Allegheny River past the village of Kittanning to meet with the French forces at what is now French Creek. Perhaps this background history was a subconscious reason I prized the hickory longbow an Indian chief gave my grandfather in the late 1800s. We shot targets with it, as we also did with his Stevens .22 rifle. He and I were great friends.

There was always talk about Grandpa Schull's grandmother, Grandma Van Tine. She was apparently a small woman, judging by the size of her rocking chair, still in our family, but her reputation made her a person of considerable stature. A century after her death, her extended family still talked about her. According to Grandpa, she had a library in German that she had brought from Europe in the early 1800s. In addition to the small rocker, a cherry chest of drawers belonging to her still serves as a splendid dining room sideboard. What belonged to her four generations ago is now in my possession, and sensing this makes Grandma Van Tine also someone to whom I belong.

Closer in time is my mother, who was musically talented and who studied music in Pittsburgh in her late teens. For a while she taught piano, even after her mother, living next door, suffered a disabling stroke. Grandma Schull continued to live for some years, and my mother made half a dozen trips a day across the yard to care for this helpless woman.

She was the perfect mother in every way. I honor her for her endless patience, her love and concern for her large extended family, and of course her care for my sister and me. After Dad was killed in an auto accident in 1930, she resumed her piano teaching to support the family and did so until her seventies. She lived until age eighty-seven, this woman to whom I belong in precious memory.

As for my father, his loving, forgiving, and generous nature made everyone else seem cold, callous, and vengeful by comparison. He championed the causes and rights of two Chinese children who were ridiculed in one of his grade schools. He improved the status of Polish scrubwomen in his buildings. He spoke out for salary increases for his teachers. During the 1918 flu epidemic he went to the Brady's Bend coal mining community an hour or two away; he had learned that the Eastern European miners there were dying like flies owing to the total lack of medical facilities. With the help of a practical nurse he set up a hospital in a former dance hall, carried sick miners from their huts to the hospital, cooked their meals, conducted Sunday services, and buried the dead. He did all this on his own initiative and funding, under no compulsion except the one inside him he could not deny.

If ever in my life I have done anything for anyone, it was because of my father's example and spirit. At the time his self-sacrificing deeds did not seem exceptional. Was not every father like that? But over the years my father's example played an ever-larger role in my choices and decisions. Obviously, more than with any other person in my life, I claim a belonging relationship to him.

My later extended family included such earthly saints as Henry Sloane Coffin, president of Union Theological Seminary in New York, and the distinguished philosopher theologian Reinhold Niebuhr. Both these men expanded my personal and spiritual horizons considerably at the same time as they stretched me in a dozen ways. They were my teachers, mentors, friends.

My sense of belonging differs in detail and content from that of everyone else—it has to, given my town's history and geography and my family makeup, personality, and later formative experiences. Fortunate are those who have a similar or equivalent sense of belonging, or can yet develop one.

The accusation is often made that old folks live in the past, that as they grow older they look back more and more to earlier years, often glorifying them out of recognition. Some say that people do this to escape the harsh realities of the experience of aging today.

That is only part of the story. Looking back can be an entirely healthy exercise. After all, we are the totality of what we have been. The earlier victories and defeats, the good deeds and the bad, are still with us, only slightly below the surface. To see ourselves as we are, to see ourselves as realistically as Dr. Maslow's choice people do, is usually to give ourselves passing grades.

We have been survivors, if not conquerors, of everything we have met so far, and thus we can look back over life with some satisfaction. Although it may not have been as good as it ought to have been, it was not as bad as it might have been. Our past is all we have available to determine what counted most in our lifetime. Out of this healthy backward look can come a new appreciation of what life basically has been for us. We can begin to see to what rich and rare causes, to what people and goals, we have belonged. Then we can reach out to that to which we legitimately belong—and claim it!

6
Sex, Sexuality, Sensuality, Love

For many people the words sex, sexuality, sensuality, and love are synonyms; they have the same meaning. Are not they all connected with our emotions, our physical urges, our bodies?

Such persons suffer from a narrow range of feeling and experience. These words can cover almost everything from brutal rape to the highest expression of human love. To make them mean the same is to distort them, raising the purely physical to an elevated plane while lowering the higher emotions to a merely physical experience.

"Sex" means the character of being female or male, all the things that distinguish women and men from each other. It covers everything connected with sexual gratification. It is physical, but under the proper circumstances it can approach the higher levels of spirituality. It is involved in the confused fumbling of teenagers, in creating a child, and in the love feast of a long-married couple.

"Sexuality" is the inborn feeling of attraction between men and women. It can lead to sexual intercourse, whether brutal or exalted, or it can be merely a strong feeling of attraction to a person of the opposite sex. The state of being sexual is common to us all, but its expression can range from the sublime feeling of Dante for Beatrice through the procreation of children to gang rape.

As defined by Robert N. Butler in *Sex After Sixty*, sexuality is "the physical and emotional responsiveness to sexual stimuli; [it] goes beyond the sex urge and the sex act."[1] It speaks of both passion and affection. It touches every level of human life. It fine-tunes the senses. The physical body takes on a touch of the spiritual, and the spiritual finds expression through human flesh. It emphasizes the present and points to the future. It refines the everyday and elevates it to the level of high hopes and aspirations. Through it the living pass from life to a kind of death and back again. It is the finest expression of intimacy. It is romance at its best.

"Sensuality," on the other hand, means the capacity for feeling not only our sexuality but also all stimuli from our senses. It shows itself by a fondness for a broad spectrum of sensual pleasures. It could take the form of purely physical or sexual pleasures, or it could lead to an overwhelming sense of a rose's beauty or the wonder of a newborn child. As an inner quality, experienced through art or music, for example, it highlights human feelings. Sensuality can take the human being beyond both the drives of the body and the workings of the mind.

"Love," in today's casual use of the word, is applied to almost everything: "I love the Dodgers," "Make love, not war," "I love you, my dear wife of fifty years." As a term for genuine emotion, it is usually used to describe the deep feelings between family members or between men and women. Recently it has also been used to describe erotic relationships between two males or two females. Love on a high level may include physical sex, but it can range far beyond physical expression to the realities of affection, abiding respect, devotion, dedication, common goals. Love, said Antoine de Saint Exupéry, does not consist in gazing at each other but in looking outward together at the same object of devotion. "Love makes the world go round," according to the old saying. Sex keeps the world populated, but love gives it quality and meaning.

Some will ask, "Why discuss sex and all its expressions in a book for older people? At their age, aren't they beyond all that?"

This assumption is based on a cruel myth that only

recently has been exploded. We now recognize that the exquisite pleasure of sex is not to be enjoyed by young people only. Older folk can and do engage in sexual intercourse with passion, satisfaction, and pleasure.

This may come as a shock to some younger people who believe their fathers and mothers are "above" such acts. How they feel is satirized in the title of a recent book, *My Parents Never Had Sex,* by Doris B. Hammond.[2] One wonders if these young people ever gave a thought as to how they came into the world. The bumper sticker reading I'M NOT A DIRTY OLD MAN. I'M A SEXY SENIOR CITIZEN comes nearer the reality.

Dozens of recent books proclaim what older people have always known: there is sex after sixty—and often far beyond! Gerontologists, psychologists, and psychiatrists, in learned journals as well as in popular books and magazines, explode the ancient myth of sexless seniors, quoting statements by older people themselves. Alfred Kinsey, who shocked society forty years ago by reporting his studies of sex as actually practiced by men and women, later narrowed his research to concentrate on the continued sex life of older people.

More recently, William H. Masters and Virginia E. Johnson have continued this research through both clinical studies and interviews.[3] There can no longer be any question about the reality of a sexual life for older people.

The sexual revolution of the sixties influenced many people who are now in their mature years. As George Leonard wrote in *Esquire,*[4] it had its good points and its bad points; it released men and women from the hush-hush "sex-is-dirty" feeling, but at the same time it tended to make sex a plaything, a recreational tool, something far removed from affection and genuine humanity. However, some of today's older people may have been rescued from the earlier Victorian view of sex by this revolution of the sixties.

It is likely that today's seniors take a broader and less-repressed view of sex than did earlier generations. It is also likely that for most of them the whole spectrum of sex involves empathy, comradeship, love, fulfillment, and intimacy rather than mere recreation or sport.

Along with changing perspectives on sex, there has been a revolution in attitudes and practice concerning divorce and remarriage on the part of older men and women. While some couples still celebrate their fiftieth wedding anniversary, less than 3 percent of all married couples today will live to celebrate half a century of marriage. When older couples are asked how long they have been married, the answer may often be three, five, or ten years. They are in their second or third marriage, after having been widowed or divorced.

Both divorce and remarriage are now socially acceptable. Fifty years ago, when a wife died, the surviving man seldom remarried. When he did, it was usually because he wished to have someone take care of his children; sometimes the man married his housekeeper for the sake of appearances. One possible reason for fewer second marriages in those days was that men and women, then having a much shorter life expectancy, might have thought that a second marriage would not be worthwhile since it was not likely to last very long.

The rate of divorce among the elderly has increased three times faster than the growth of the older population as a whole. Of those who divorce, 80 percent remarry, and half of second marriages end in divorce. As someone has remarked, these divorces do not indicate a cynicism about love and marriage, but only that the particular spouse is not satisfactory. Perhaps the next one will be! Hope springs eternal in the human breast, we are told, no matter what the age.

Because younger couples today have a more casual attitude toward both marriage and divorce, we can expect the rate of divorce among older people to increase a few decades from now. Moreover, what is happening now to men and women in their twenties and thirties is also taking place with people sixty years of age and above: more divorces, more remarriages, but also more live-in couples. It is likely that the present trend will not only continue but escalate.

Women remarrying usually look for a different type of man. Their first husband may have been suitable as a breadwinner and father of their children. They are more likely to select a second or third spouse on the basis of companionship, love, and romance. An older newlywed of either sex will probably have chosen a new mate on the basis of shared social, leisure, and intellectual interests.

Another factor that cannot be overlooked is the shifting ratio of men and women. A half century ago, men usually outlived their wives. The situation has now been reversed. Today women live longer than men, and thus there are far more women than men in all older age brackets. Furthermore, the older decades have an increasingly smaller number of men. Therefore, older women have increasingly less access to men as sex or marriage partners.

For every 100 women ages 65 to 69, there are 81 men of that age. There are 72 men for every 100 women at ages 70 to 74, 63 men at ages 75 to 79, 53 men at ages 80 to 84, 43 men at ages 85 to 89, 36 men at ages 90 to 94, 32 men at ages 95 to 99, and 30 men age 100 or over.[5]

The number of people living alone also indicates a greater number of women than men. At ages 65 to 74, 34 percent of women live alone compared to 12 percent of men. At ages 75 to 84, 51 percent of women live alone, compared to 23 percent of men. At age 85 and over, 52 percent of women live alone, compared to 29 percent of men.[6]

This chapter's encouraging picture of sexuality, sex, and love obviously does not take into account the fact that women outlive men and that the unbalanced sex ratio makes marriage or cohabitation impossible for many older women.

For older people who do have partners, there can be the "second language of sex," as Robert Butler suggests in *Sex After Sixty*. The first language is that of youthful passion and the procreation of children. Then, as years of maturity come, there is sex for its own sake: pleasure, release, communication, shared intimacy, romance.

If we want to move in new directions in our personal life, the second language of sex has a good deal to offer us: "shared tenderness, warmth, humor, merriment, anger, passion, sorrow, camaraderie."[7]

As Butler puts it,

> Perhaps only in the later years can life with its various possibilities have the chance to shape itself into something approximating a human work of art. And perhaps only in later life, when personality reaches its final stages of development, can love-making and sex achieve the fullest possible growth. Sex does not merely exist after sixty; it holds the possibility of becoming greater than it ever was. It can be joyful and creative, healthy and health-giving. It unites human beings in an affirmation of love and is therefore also morally right and virtuous.[8]

The extensive literature about the sex life of older people points out that when sexual activity is no longer possible, disuse invariably is the culprit. All sex performance for older men ends when, over a protracted period, there is no use of the sex organ. However, the practice of masturbation by some men keeps their sexual powers intact. Likewise, for women, sexual inactivity over a number of years leads to physical changes in the sex organ. On the other hand, there is solid evidence that most men and women can have an active and satisfying sex life even in their eighties if there has been continuity.

Dr. Alfred J. Levenson of Houston, Texas, speaking at an aging conference, emphasized that people in their sixties and seventies, even in their eighties, should have an active sex life, although special medical or surgical problems may prevent this in some circumstances. Of course, he said, the man who has had no sexual intercourse in his early sixties should not expect to awaken on his sixty-fifth birthday with a strong sexual drive!

Levenson affirmed what all recent gerontologists have been saying and what this book also affirms: that life can be an ongoing, continually expanding, growing, enlarging entity. Increased years should not diminish it but should help us develop a larger and richer life—and this includes life's sexual side.

7

Expand Your Spiritual Well-being

Everything in our lives is inextricably tied together and fashioned into a workable whole by the spiritual forces within and around us. Our bodies and minds, by themselves, cannot create a fully rounded human being. Without spiritual undergirding, you and I are like a three-legged stool lacking one leg. Our total person can function only when body, mind, and spirit support and sustain one another. The body by itself is merely a physical machine; the spirit all alone becomes a disembodied, ghostlike apparition; the mind separate unto itself is powerless. Only all three, in harmony, can make a perfect human being, a satisfaction to the self and a blessing to the world. We have the potential for becoming such a being!

Those who are ignorant or neglectful of their spiritual well-being rarely enjoy a serene and fulfilled life. Certainly, older men and women who fear death suffer from a serious spiritual deficiency. They lack the believer's trust and assurance, and into this vacuum flow uncertainty, fear, and terror.

The Swiss psychologist Carl G. Jung, writing in *Modern Man in Search of a Soul*, stated that the problem of all of his patients in the second half of life was, in the last resort, that of finding a religious outlook on life.[1] As he saw it, his older patients lacked spiritual orientation.

On the other hand, overwhelming evidence exists to show that the ills to which human flesh is heir, including the consciousness of inevitable death, cannot destroy the equanimity, confidence, and trust of those who have a sustaining spiritual life.

Many elderly people show remarkable courage, zest, and vision in surviving our competitive, sometimes inhospitable, youth- and beauty-oriented society. What keeps them going? It seems clear that what sustains them through personal losses, physical deterioration, and insecurity about the future are the inner resources at their command.

The question can be raised as to whether religion and spirituality are two terms for the same reality. They can be, of course, and perhaps for many people they are synonymous. "Religion" usually refers to formal religious institutional observances, to what takes place in an organized church or synagogue. On the other hand, "spirituality" suggests a personal relationship with the God of one's soul or with unseen and unnamed forces in the universe and in one's own self.

Spirituality may be associated with a specific religious institution or it may not. Some older people have moved beyond the limits of organized religion; for them, formal religion seems to stand in the way of finding a satisfying life of the spirit. Sometimes religious practices inhibit spiritual growth. The Pharisees in Jesus' day were concerned only with the letter of the law and not its spirit. For most people today, however, spirituality is found in and through a serious involvement in churches, synagogues, and other religious societies and institutions.

Roy W. Fairchild has defined spirituality as "one's unique and personal response to the call of Christ through the Spirit, in the world of inner and outer realities." For the Christian, this means "God is in the very midst of us, in the very fabric of our lives, in all dimensions." Spirituality is expressed in the here and now, related to everyday life and its needs.[2]

Native Americans possess a rich heritage of the spirit that undergirds and supports them. Their spirituality emphasizes the totality of all things; the unity of life, the relation of everything in their world to everything else, seen and unseen. Their sense of the Great Spirit touches all levels of existence, even that of their ancestors.

Popovi Da, a noted potter and tribal leader and the son of Maria Martinez, the renowned creator of Indian pottery at the San Idelfonso pueblo in northern New Mexico, has said this: "Our symbols and our ceremonial representations are all expressed as an endless cadence, and beautifully organized in our art as well as our dance.

"There is a design in human beings; their shapes, forms, the ability to live. All have meaning. . . . Our values are indwelling and dependent upon time and space unmeasured. This in itself is beauty."[3]

Recently we have had many other interpretations of spirituality. Shirley MacLaine, in *Out on a Limb*[4] and other books, has reported mystical and spiritual encounters, both in-body and out-of-body. Millions of people in our day have experienced various expressions of spirituality through transcendental meditation, Zen, and variations of Eastern religions. These expressions, not normally found in churches and synagogues, have given millions of people a sense of what an experience of the spirit can mean in one's life.

However found, the spiritual dimension of life should dominate one's entire being and should constitute one's main life force. According to Leo E. Missinne, professor of gerontology at the University of Nebraska, "It is as basic a need as our biological need for food, air, and water, and as our psychological need for love and social interaction." The Belgian priest continues, "For the elderly especially [it is] the search for meaning in life."[5]

What may be considered an authoritative definition of spiritual well-being is that of the National Interfaith Coalition on Aging (NICA), an agency set up by Protestant, Jewish, and Catholic bodies:

> The *Spiritual* is not one dimension among many in life; rather, it permeates and gives meaning to all life. The term Spiritual Well-Being, therefore, indicates wholeness in contrast to fragmentation and isolation. "Spiritual" connotes our dependence on the source of life, God the Creator.[6]

Above all, spirituality is an affirmation of life. It declares that life is good despite pain and suffering. It is an expression of the value one attributes to one's own life. Going beyond one's self, it expresses a deep concern for humankind's struggle for peace, justice, and equality. Spirituality creates in us a deep concern about the whole human race.

Spiritual well-being, as the NICA statement makes plain, comes through individual initiative and concern—but never in a vacuum. What counts is the interaction between the person and other people and the larger community. It is never found once and for all but is a growing, becoming, developing condition, which adapts itself to one's life and one's needs. This inner force is what we make it, and it is what it makes us.

What are the components of spiritual well-being? The three important elements of reverence, commitment, and gratitude are important to older persons.

Reverence. Fifty or sixty years ago, Boy Scouts took a pledge to be "reverent." How much that meant to us is questionable; we probably associated it with something about church and gave it little thought at the time. A half century later, what does reverence mean to us? If we have been sensitive and aware of life around us, we have seen that it has a meaning far beyond our earlier conception and is related to all of life.

Reverence touches our appreciation of human love. It colors our attitude toward the beauty of the world around us. Going beyond this, we sense the sublimity and infinite mystery of the human species, especially in that marvel of all marvels, our body, and above all in the miracle of the human mind.

The mark of our maturity may well be the degree to which we sense reverence: that is, revering, bowing before, opening ourselves up, allowing unseen influences to touch us, having a feeling of awe and wonder, a sense of veneration for life and all who are living. To be reverent is to have ultimate respect for the divine in us and the holy in everything around us.

Ralph Waldo Emerson, the sage of Concord in the

nineteenth century, was asked why he, a great thinker and writer of world renown, still went to a small, not very significant church for Sunday services. He answered, "There is a plant in the corner of my heart called reverence which needs watering about once a week."

A man different in many ways from Emerson was Albert Einstein. Not religious in the conventional sense of the word, he wrote:

> It is enough for me to contemplate the mystery of conscious life perpetuating itself through all eternity, to reflect upon the marvelous structure of the universe which we can dimly perceive, and to try humbly to comprehend even an infinitesimal part of the intelligence manifested in nature.... The most beautiful thing we can experience is the mysterious. It is the source of all true art and science. He to whom this emotion is a stranger, who can no longer pause to wonder and stand rapt in awe, is as good as dead.... To know that what is impenetrable to us really exists, manifesting itself as the highest wisdom and the most radiant beauty which our dull faculties can comprehend only in their most primitive forms—this knowledge, this feeling, is at the center of true religiousness.[7]

For all of us, a feeling of wonder and mystery is essential. It opens up to us the fullest meaning of life around us. It keeps us ever on the alert for new truth. We are always conscious that there is more to be learned, more to be explored, more to be attained. We are challenged to learn more, and thus we do learn more. A new creativity is born in us. The noted art critic John Ruskin once remarked, "The whole difference between a man of genius and other men ... is that the first remains in great part a child, seeing with the large eyes of children, in perpetual wonder."

Commitment. A sense of spirituality is the acknowledgment that a power beyond one's self exists and is in control. It is a readiness to surrender to the sovereignty of this power, to acknowledge its reality, and to put one's self in touch with it. There is a childlike straightforwardness about it all.

Involved in this commitment is a simple trust, as we see in

the familiar words of Job: "Though he slay me, yet will I trust in him" (Job 13:15, KJV). It is both the naïve trust of a small child and the total submission to a superior power of a wise, mature person.

The world's great religions feature this giving in, this giving over. The followers of Muhammad surrender themselves to Allah, the name they give to God. The name of their religion, Islam, means "submission." Having no question about the nature of their deity, they put themselves without qualification in the control of Allah and submit to his will in all things.

At the heart of Christianity there is also a submission to God. Christians speak of "commitment," a voluntary giving over of one's self to a loving, superior power. The personal devotions of many Christians focus upon Jesus' last words on the cross: "Father, into thy hands I commit my spirit" (Luke 23:46). They remember also his prayer in the Garden of Gethsemene: "Not my will, but thine, be done" (Luke 22:42). Following such faith is to go into the unknown areas, doing what Lord Tennyson's words suggest, "believing where we cannot prove."[8]

This commitment means seeking always to do the will of God—first to seek it out and then to do it as well as we can. This often takes us into deep waters, perhaps leading us into public positions at odds with our contemporaries, especially when the social change we advocate would alter society in a way others oppose.

The consciousness of this inner power leads people of mature years to undertake deeds of mercy and acts of human service, often more than in any earlier period of their lives. In doing so, they set an example for younger men and women to reach out in service to the handicapped and needy in their communities.

Gratitude. Spiritual well-being should show in our faces. The joy of living, the zest for life, the pleasure in living out one's days in a world of beauty and meaning—these should be apparent in everything we say and do and are. Our deep gratitude to the Great Spirit should be obvious to others as they see the look in our eyes, the posture of our bodies, the spring in our step. If this is not the way you and I are, certainly we have known people like this. This is the way every mature child of God should be.

To be moved by the power of this silent force within us is to have body and mind in perfect coordination, to have a life of balance and grace and charm. In work and in play, alone or with others, we instinctively live out our faith in all of its dimensions. We do not have to work hard to be this way; soon it comes naturally. There is a sense of completion in our lives as we say with Augustine, "Our souls are restless till they find their rest in Thee."

Of course not all of us are like this. The years have exacted their toll. Life has laid on its harsh blows. Through our actions we unconsciously speak more about our failures than our triumphs. Gratitude is not an emotion that overwhelms us. However, we older people obviously have much for which to be thankful. We have survived wars, depressions, and the many lesser blows circumstances have foisted upon us. Isn't it good to be alive, to have come through life's adversities? Even to be a survivor these days is reason to rejoice. Many of those we started with earlier in life did not make it.

What is essential is to review our lives. To look backward honestly is to call to mind the days and years of satisfaction, achievement, love, intense pleasure, praise received, and work accomplished with a satisfactory outcome. We recall victories over illness, the joys of childhood, the love and affection of family and friends, sunsets and full moons, the beauty of earth and flowers, and the delight of children. Many times we were able to accomplish tasks that at the beginning had seemed impossible.

Above all, we should listen to the saints and explorers of life, the ancient writers of scripture, the modern interpreters of religion, the philosophers, poets, and others who over the centuries found life rich and fine, despite the "slings and arrows of outrageous fortune." No book ever made would be massive enough to contain all the paeans of praise, the expressions of delight, the shouts of joy uttered by people very much like us who rejoiced in the good gift of life.

A British novelist of a generation ago, John Cowper Powys, writing at age seventy-two (he lived to be ninety), reminds us of the wonder of every day: "We poor dullards of habit and custom, we besotted and befuddled takers of life for granted, require the hell of a flaming thunderbolt to raise us to the fact that every single second of conscious life is a miracle past reckoning, a marvel past all computation."[9]

Countless millions have in their own way expressed the same delight in simply being alive. One likes to think they had some inner power of the spirit causing them to treasure every waking moment. They may not have been conscious of exercising such a power. They were merely expressing the gift of spirituality with which all of us to a degree are blessed through our heritage as human beings created in the image of God.

My own feeling of joie de vivre expresses itself in a variety of ways. It clearly affects my view of death. How could the extinction of my life lead into anything other than something equally breathtaking? If life is the delight I have found it to be, can any circumstance that follows be anything basically different? Like others who have at least a touch of the eternal spirit in them, I do not fear death. It holds no terrors for me. I have faith that a loving God will do with me whatever is best for me. What that will be I have not the slightest idea.

Will there be punishment for my sins or reward for my virtues? I do not know. I never think about it. My attitude may suggest that of Teresa of Avila, who is said to have walked the city streets with a flaming torch and a bucket of water. She cried out, "With the torch I shall set fire to Heaven, and with the water I shall quench the fires of Hell, so that I can love God for Himself alone." For me the word is trust as much as love.

My only regret as I contemplate the end of my present existence is that it will not be possible to pass on to anyone my great joy in living, the marvel of it all, the feeling about life expressed by John Cowper Powys.

How can I bequeath to anyone—wife, sister, children, grandchildren, friends—the intense, life-enhancing appreciation of art, music, literature, and the beauty of the world around me? I have always cherished the words of Edna St. Vincent Millay:

> Lord, I do fear
> Thou'st made the world too beautiful this year;
> My soul is all but out of me,—let fall
> No burning leaf; prithee, let no bird call.[10]

The poet was looking at the natural world around her. Equally inspiring to me is the man-made, woman-made beauty and glory of art and poetry, great literature, the wonders of philosophy and science, magnificent music, the glory of humanity at its finest, the excitement of the beginning of each day.

It is not necessary for me to pass on anything to others, for whatever I possess is already latent in them and around them. It needs only to be recognized, appreciated, and absorbed. The great joy in living I have cherished over the years was not my own invention or my singular discovery. It came partly as a gift out of the blue, unsought, and partly out of an openness where I always tried to present to life a hunger for more! What has blessed me is available to everyone. The rich life of the spirit is there for everyone who desires it and wishes to take advantage of its silent power. This is what everyone is looking for, even though this hidden hunger may not be recognized for what it is. To employ Abraham Maslow's phrase, it is making actual one's full potential, sensing the serenity and the security of being self-actualized. This is to fulfill the finest of all human aspirations.

Spirituality is a many-sided quality of human existence. It

takes us into everything that touches our best lives. It drives our physical machine to greater usefulness and our minds into paths of contemplation and action. Rather than "elevating" us into some visionary other world, it leads us into nearby social and political action, into using our inner gifts and character to benefit the less privileged in our midst. This inner power helps us face up to life's hard choices.

The search for spiritual fulfillment does not lead us on a pilgrimage to Rome or Jerusalem or Mecca; it deals with the opportunities and challenges of the real world around us. The secret is to let ourselves go when touched with reverence, be ready to give ourselves in commitment to all that is finest in life, and in deep gratitude dedicate ourselves to the highest we know and can possibly envision.

Broadening our spiritual horizons may turn out to be the greatest challenge that older people face. In the end, it could prove to be the most satisfying.

8
Stretch Your Mind to the Limit

Increasingly, more and more is written about "extraterrestrial intelligence." Is there life in outer space? Are there beings with whom we can communicate? Are these faraway residents of distant universes seeking to communicate with us?

Such curiosity may prompt the research of scientists and their amateur followers. But what do we know about "terrestrial intelligence"—earthly intelligence? Have we explored the breadth of human mental processes? Isn't there a greater need today to use the human mind more fully?

Scientific speculation has always resulted in the growth of knowledge. This process must never end. All we know about the human species and the universe is still not enough. The human mind has no limits, nor should our present range of intelligence ever be considered final, with further search unnecessary.

The intelligence we already have should be exercised toward the betterment of human life. Not only do scientists, philosophers, and spiritual leaders have this responsibility, but also all the rest of us. This challenge pertains especially to older people in the final decade of the century. How can the age-old barriers holding back people of mature years be lifted and finally eliminated? How can further growth and development of the 30 million people over age sixty be brought about? The answer is plainly through education—further education, reeducation, continued education.

"The promise of late-life learning is nothing less than the challenge of human development in the second half of life," declared R. H. Moody of Hunter College's Brookdale Center on Aging in New York.[1] Education in later life should provide instruction, pleasurable hours, skills, and usable information, but above all it should expand human life by helping men and women realize their full potential.

Since education for older people was never before viewed as either useful or possible, it was not considered practical to educate the older generation. Thus we have never learned what advances in society could be made by men and women of mature age. Today's development in "after retirement" education could eventually result in solid contributions to the world. A generation assumed by many to be unable to do anything consequential could one day add to the storehouse of the world's knowledge.

The Elderhostel program offers an almost perfect combination of learning and travel. Since travel is both broadening and instructive, Elderhostel presents a doubly tasty menu of learning. It combines the best traditions of education and hosteling. Inspired by the youth hostels and folk schools of Europe, but guided by the needs of older citizens for travel, intellectual stimulation, and physical adventure, Elderhostel is designed for older citizens on the move. It offers not only travel but the opportunity to reach out to new experiences and broaden one's life.

Elderhostel is a nonprofit network of over a thousand colleges, universities, and independent schools in the United States and around the world that offer special low-cost, short-term, residential, academic programs to people at least sixty years of age. Places of study are as close as a nearby university or as far away as Rome, Australia, India, the Soviet Union, and Brazil, and hundreds of places in between. While attending a program, participants have access to the cultural and recreational facilities and resources available in the area.

In 1989 more than 190,000 people participated in Elderhostel programs. There were no exams, no grades, and no required homework, although the instructors were happy to guide students to further study.[2]

Travel at home or abroad and a variety of academically respectable courses make an unbeatable combination of true quality.

However, this brief experience is too soon over. It whets the appetite so that we are ready to dig in deeper, and then it comes to an end. An increasing number of older people want to go farther. This suggests college and university. And people of mature age and tastes are now flocking to institutions of higher learning.

Universities report that their student-body age average continues to go up. In my undergraduate days the average age of the student body was probably no more than twenty years. It is now over thirty in many places.

What has caused this amazing rise? Only one answer: older people are going back to school. The trickle of a generation ago has become a solid stream of older people seeking to extend their education and expand their lives.

Think what must be going on in the mind and consciousness of a woman I know, now in her middle eighties, who is taking a full undergraduate course! If she were seen in a graduation ceremony she might stand out a bit because of her white hair, but all around her would be others of fifty, sixty, or seventy. How different from 1929 when my father, then age fifty-five, received a master's degree. With his heavy body and thin hair this school principal stood out like the proverbial sore thumb. Everyone in line was three decades younger. Today he would not be noticed.

Many of today's older people are educationally deprived because they were in school fifty years or more ago when the information base was considerably smaller than it is today. For example, the physics courses I took in college would be taught in high school today. Some people also stopped their schooling four to six years earlier than young persons do today. They need to catch up.

Today's more mature student group is made up of men and women in many different circumstances. Some are seeking an undergraduate degree denied them earlier in life;

others are taking specialized courses in writing or the arts because of an overwhelming inner desire to express their creativity. Some, who may already have earned a bachelor's degree, want additional exposure to the same academic subject so they can feel more at home in a discipline long familiar to them. Others are taking an advanced degree either to satisfy a longtime desire or to prepare themselves for a second career in education, another profession, science, business, or even in diplomacy.

A Canadian friend in his mid-eighties spends his winters in Tucson, Arizona, so that he can use the research facilities of the University of Arizona to complete a book he has been working on for some time.

In my father's time there were skeptics who denied the possibility of anyone learning anything after age thirty. Learning ability peaks shortly after twenty years of age, they claimed, and then the learning curve goes down sharply. How strange that back in the 1920s my father was making top grades at age fifty-five!

Now we know that the learning curve goes down very slowly. We recognize that learning is more than a trick of memory. Teenagers can outdo septuagenarians in quick memorization—language vocabulary, for example. However, learning is far more complicated than mere memorization. It includes the ability to relate facts and events, to see the significance of what is being studied, sense the inner meanings, in light of lifetime experience. All these factors enable older persons to do well.

If older men and women are in classes with younger people who are taking courses because they have to and who are bored by the subject, they will outshine those forty or fifty years younger. For mature students, many compensating factors make up for their years. Thus, older Americans in good health should take full advantage of today's higher educational opportunities.

A friend was visiting a man who, as a widower, was living in the dormitory at the University of Washington and taking courses in American history. While they were talking, a young coed burst into the room to ask Joe something about the course. My friend learned that these two—sixty-eight and nineteen—made a perfect learning pair. She brought her eagerness and curiosity and he brought the experience of living through much of what they were studying. Youth has only part of the learning equipment essential to a total education.

Recent research offers proof that even people of advanced ages who keep involved in life and maintain good health need not suffer a decline in creativity and intellectual capacity. Warner Schaie of Penn State University has been studying 3,000 people for decades, some of them now in their eighties. "For some mental capacities," he has said, "there begin to slight declines in the 60s and more meaningful declines in the 80s. But some mental capacities decline very little, or can improve in old age." What counts is one's attitude toward life. "The expectation of a decline is a self-fulfilling prophecy. Those who do not accept the stereotype of a helpless old age, but instead feel they can do as well in old age as they have at other times of their lives, don't become ineffective before their time."[3]

Another study of this issue was made by the National Institute of Aging. Scientists there did brain scans of men ranging from twenty-one to eighty-three. They found that the healthy aging brain is as active and efficient as the healthy young brain. The conclusion was that although some brain cells are lost through the years, there are still more than enough functioning at an advanced age. It is a myth about aging that the years bring on senility. Senility is a result of brain disease, not part of the aging process.

It is significant that college towns and university cities are becoming choice retirement spots for educationally minded older people. As Ken Dychtwald reports in *Age Wave*,

> Instead of Sun City and Leisure World, towns such as Eugene, Oregon; Madison, Wisconsin; Austin, Texas; Ann Arbor,

Michigan; Williamstown, Massachusetts; Ithaca, New York; Burlington, Vermont; Annapolis, Maryland; Charlottesville, Virginia; Hanover, New Hampshire; and Chapel Hill and Winston-Salem, North Carolina, are beginning to see a significant growth in the number of older immigrants who want to be in the middle of, not removed from, the action.[4]

The evidence is clear: more older people feel the need and worth of additional education in a wide variety of fields. They are returning in large numbers to colleges and universities for special courses or for a degree. Just as American public schools formed the basis of our country's development, institutions of higher learning are now providing opportunities for older people to achieve a more fulfilling life.

The noted tenor Luciano Pavarotti related an incident in his youth. As a budding opera singer, he had an interview with the leading concert and operatic star of the day, a man then fifty-seven years old. While waiting inside the star's house he could hear the noted singer practicing. Later, while talking with him, Pavarotti asked him how long he had studied. "Until ten minutes ago," he answered. Pavarotti later remarked that this was the most important singing lesson of his career: Studying never ends.

This fits into the "lifelong learner" concept now accepted as absolutely fundamental for today's older people. The evidence is clear: either we learn more or soon we know less; we advance or we fall back. We now recognize this maxim as an immutable law of life—long life. We should continue the learning process as long as we live, or as long as we want to stay alive!

As the older generation increases in numbers and the younger generation becomes proportionally smaller, there will be more quality work opportunities for people at or past retirement age. With the need for skilled and experienced workers at all levels of society, "retirement" as a category may have to be abolished. The services of older people will be in great demand.

What is the best use we can make of our awakened

intellect? Apart from preparing for possible vocational opportunities ahead, there is always the excellent alternative of achieving an additional familiarity with the liberal arts. Study in this field can always be fulfilling to the mature mind.

A very satisfying adventure for many older people is to become knowledgeable about some important issue or concern. There are various subjects that touch us and our times. If taken seriously, such an effort can make us authorities in the field, if only in our own eyes. One beauty of this kind of project is that we can get into it merely enough to get our feet wet or, with more involvement, swim in deep water.

Among the various studies one can undertake, the three that follow have their own distinctive attractiveness. Two of them enlarge our understanding of our democratic heritage and thus make us more enlightened citizens, while the third helps us take a special look at ourselves.

The Constitution of the United States. The drafting of the U.S. Constitution, its adoption by the thirteen colonies, and the addition of the Bill of Rights compose one of the outstanding events of human history. That the colonial leaders of a small, recently freed colony on the edge of a vast unknown continental wilderness could produce a document of this eminence was an astounding feat. That the Constitution could endure for two centuries, guiding the nation in its destiny and also being an inspiration to people around the world, is, even when seen in retrospect, an almost impossible achievement. (See the list of readings at the end of this chapter.)

Roger Williams. An alternate study of the nation's beginnings could center on Roger Williams. Founder of Rhode Island and defender of the area's Indians, Williams had been in England the friend of statesmen Sir Edward Coke and Sir Henry Vane and the poet-agitator John Milton. He believed in and practiced democracy far more than his contemporaries in the Massachusetts Bay Colony.

In the mid-1600s, long before Thomas Jefferson was born, Roger Williams preached and practiced the civil, religious, and political rights set forth in the Bill of Rights almost a century and a half later. He abhorred all qualifications for citizenship based on religious, ethnic, or other labels. To the Rhode Island community he welcomed people of all races and religions—atheist, Jew, Hindu, and Quaker. His colony sheltered refugees of conscience from the Massachusetts Bay Colony. He treated the Narragansett Indians as equals, not only dealing with them fairly and humanely but also learning their language. More than any other person of his time or later, this good Christian made clear the absolute necessity of total religious liberty. He was a late-twentieth-century man three and a half centuries ahead of his time. Surely he was the first father of his country. (See the list of readings.)

Self-Knowledge. For you and me to see ourselves clearly, we need to look at our lives, our advanced years, our ideas, and our identity from a gerontological perspective. This is one way to "know thyself," as the ancient Greek teaching would have us do. Self-knowledge is basic to all other knowledge, for without knowing oneself it is impossible to know other people or evaluate human events. Certainly one is not able to make the most of science, philosophy, and other intellectual disciplines.

What better thing can we do than learn about ourselves, both as persons and as members of today's very special older generation? To do so is not to seek knowledge for its own sake but to find a knowledge that explains ourselves to ourselves, that sets forth the limitations of age as well as its many positive factors. Such a study details the physical, emotional, and intellectual changes we undergo as we get older, as well as showing us how to handle them.

The more we know about ourselves, the more we shall be proud to be our present age—and to profit by it. (See the list of suggested readings.)

Who can foresee what blessings to the world will one day come about through the development and utilization of the minds and talents of the older generation! A genuinely wise society will cultivate and put to use the mature intelligence of these experienced men and women.

Suggested Reading

On the Constitution

Bowen, Catherine Drinker. *The Miracle at Philadelphia.* Boston: Little, Brown & Co., 1986.

———. *The Most Dangerous Man in America: Scenes from the Life of Benjamin Franklin.* Boston: Little, Brown & Co., 1986.

Bowers, Claude G. *Jefferson and Hamilton.* Irvine, Calif.: Reprint Service Corp. Reprint of 1925 ed.

Brandt, Irving. *The Fourth President: A Life of James Madison.* Indianapolis: Bobbs-Merrill Co., 1970.

Flexner, James Thomas. *Washington: The Indispensable Man.* New York: New American Library, 1984. A condensation of his four-volume life of Washington.

Kammen, Michael. *A Machine That Would Go of Itself: The Constitution in American Culture.* New York: Random House, 1987.

Ketcham, Ralph Louis. *James Madison: A Biography.* New York: Macmillan Publishing Co., 1971.

Malone, Dumas. *Jefferson and His Time* (vol. 6 of 6 vol. series of this name). Boston: Little, Brown & Co., 1982.

———. *Jefferson and the Rights of Man* (vol. 2), 1968.

———. *Jefferson the President: Second Term, 1805–1809* (vol. 5), 1975.

Peters, William. *A More Perfect Union.* New York: Crown Publishers, 1987.

Also see articles on Washington, Jefferson, and the Constitution in the *Encyclopedia Britannica.*

On Roger Williams

Brockunier, Samuel Hugh. *The Irrepressible Democrat, Roger Williams.* New York: Ronald Press, 1940.

Chupack, Henry. *Roger Williams.* New York: Twayne Publishers, 1969.
Covey, Cyclone. *The Gentle Radical: A Biography of Roger Williams.* New York: Macmillan Co., 1966.
Miller, Perry. *Roger Williams: His Contribution to the American Tradition.* Indianapolis: Bobbs-Merrill Co., 1953; reprint 1962.
Morgan, Edmund S. *Roger Williams—The Church and State.* New York: Harcourt, Brace & World, 1967.
Parrington, Vernon L. *The Colonial Mind.* New York: Harcourt, Brace & Co., 1954; pp. 62–75.
Winslow, Ola Elizabeth. *Master Roger Williams.* New York: Macmillan Co., 1957.
See also the article on Williams in the *Encyclopedia Britannica.*

On Self-knowledge

Atchley, Robert G. *Social Forces and Aging* (5th ed.). Belmont, Calif.: Wadsworth Publishing Co., 1988.
Beauvoir, Simone de. *Coming of Age.* New York: G. P. Putnam's Sons, 1972.
Butler, Robert N. *Why Survive? Being Old In America.* New York: Harper & Row, Torchbooks, 1985.
Carter, Jimmy, and Rosalynn Carter. *Everything to Gain: Making the Most of the Rest of Your Life.* New York: Random House, 1987.
Cox, Harold, ed. *Aging* (6th ed.). Guilford, Conn.: Dushkin Publishing Co., 1989.
Dangott, Lillian R. and Richard A. Kalish. *A Time to Enjoy: The Pleasures of Aging.* Englewood Cliffs, N.J.: Prentice-Hall, 1979.
Doress, Paula Brown, and Diana Laskin Siega. *Ourselves, Growing Older.* New York: Simon & Schuster, 1988.
Dychtwald, Ken, and Joe Flower. *Age Wave.* Los Angeles: Jeremy P. Tarcher, 1989.
Fischer, David Hackett. *Growing Old in America.* New York: Oxford University Press, 1978.

Huyck, Margaret Hellie. *Growing Older.* Englewood Cliffs, N.J.: Prentice-Hall, 1974.

Jones, Maxwell. *Growing Old—The Ultimate Freedom.* New York: Human Sciences Press, 1988.

Kaufman, Sharon R. *The Ageless Self.* New York: New American Library, 1987.

Luce, Gay. *Your Second Life: Vitality in Middle and Later Age.* New York: Delacorte Press, 1979.

Pifer, Alden, and Lydia Bronte, eds. *Our Aging Society: Paradox and Promise.* New York: W. W. Norton & Co., 1986.

Scott-Maxwell, Florida. *The Measure of My Days.* New York: Penguin Books, 1979.

Skinner, B. F., and Margaret Vaughan. *Enjoying Old Age.* New York: W. W. Norton & Co., 1983.

Tournier, Paul. *Learn to Grow Old.* New York: Harper & Row, 1972.

9

Seek to Broaden Your World

Food, shelter, water, air, and sleep are sufficient to keep the human animal alive. These are not enough, however, to enable us to live at much more than an animal level. Personal associations, work, and belief in a Supreme Being elevate *Homo sapiens* still another notch. However, to reach fulfillment as persons distinct from the animal kingdom, men and women require the refining touches of music, literature, and the arts. Planned travel experience adds an extra touch of grace.

What has been painted, sculpted, written, played, or sung for at least ten thousand years of human history is important for us and our times. Although books and the written record do not reach quite as far back in the centuries, they pass on to us the wisdom and experience of the ages. We are the poorer if we ignore or neglect them. The philosopher George Santayana once remarked that those who are ignorant of the past are destined to repeat its mistakes. They are also destined to miss humanity's great moments, history's teaching experience, and the potential for mature development.

Not everything of value has to be old. In our day some people look with suspicion, if not hostility, upon modern art and modern music, and even upon some contemporary literature. However, modern literature speaks richly about the human condition. Modern art calls on us to reach the questions deep within ourselves and reflect on possible answers about our age and generation. Modern music touches both our minds and our emotions. They are for us what the visual and plastic arts were for earlier generations of the human race.

We can find new insights by examining some works that many people do not readily accept. For example, *Ulysses* by James Joyce is hard to understand. However, if we read his *Portrait of the Artist as a Young Man,* written earlier, we will find a novel of surpassing quality in language familiar to us all. Later in his career Joyce felt the commonly accepted English language was inadequate for him, and thus he had to go beyond current usage. You and I might find it worth our time and effort to explore his later form of expression. The mature Joyce can be no more difficult to read than Shakespeare, whose words are also often unfamiliar to us. Just as the Bard pushed drama beyond its then-known limits, so this great Irish writer expanded the English language.

The same thing can be said about the artist Pablo Picasso. His 1890s paintings of his mother and sister are exceptionally fine portraits. But, like Joyce, he eventually felt that he had to go beyond the limits of conventional painting. "Why not paint the interior of a woman at the same time her outside form is depicted?" he might have asked. He attempted just this with several famous paintings.

Ours is the most inventive age in history, and everyone marvels at our mechanical and scientific innovations and our space explorations. How strange that new and bold expressions in the field of the arts do not receive equal admiration!

The great musical compositions of the seventeenth, eighteenth, and nineteenth centuries fascinate us. We hail the work of Bach, Beethoven, Schubert, Mozart, and the great Russian composers. Does that mean that modern composers should copy the music of these early masters? To do so would not be honest or creative. These great men did not copy their predecessors.

Perhaps people do not always realize that everything Mozart and Beethoven wrote and performed was modern to their contemporaries. When Mozart performed in Paris, he would not repeat the symphony or concerto he had presented the week before in Prague. In the eighteenth century the public everywhere demanded new and fresh works. How often do you recall that Beethoven's majestic Ninth Symphony was modern music, something recently composed, at its first performance? For his hearers it was contemporary music.

To further confuse our views of what is modern and what is classical, consider *Death and the Maiden* by Franz Schubert. Written in 1825, its style was a full century premature. It was considered so dissonant at the time that no publisher would touch it. *Death and the Maiden* was published only after Schubert's death. The history of this work turns upside down the usual ideas of what "classical" and "modern" mean.

In our modern world everything must be in today's latest style—clothing, architecture, cars, hairdos—almost everything but art and music. How contradictory! What a loss!

In most cases ignorance of and unfamiliarity with the arts causes them to be disdained. William Lyon Phelps of Yale University, an arbiter of taste in contemporary literature of the 1930s, helped a wide audience come to greater appreciation of books of that day. In one of a series of pamphlets he described how he came to appreciate classical music.

While still a young university student, he was invited to attend a symphony concert. He went to it with great expectations, but without much background in music appreciation. When he heard the opening bars from the orchestra, he was stunned. What horrible sounds were tearing at his eardrums! He looked around him, expecting to see everyone else in shock, protest, and revolt. Much to his amazement he saw looks of delight and pleasure on people's faces. An intelligent man, he came to an instant conclusion: either these other people were wrong in their reactions, or he was. So he decided to listen openly and with possible appreciation. In the end, classical music became as important to him as literature.

What happened to him with classical music can happen to people today with all the arts if they are ready to open themselves to the impact of modern artistic creations. The problem may be an unfamiliarity with the works, not a defect in the works themselves.

Reading Phelps's pamphlet more than forty years ago led me to listen to dissonant music by Stravinsky and others. This approach to new cultural expressions opened me up to modern art, even the most outrageous and shocking. The result? My appreciation was broadened and gave me greater pleasure and deeper understanding. I came to feel quite secure in rejecting the absurd, while cherishing the pieces I carried away in my memory.

As the Phelps story suggests about music, art works deserve serious attention. I learned to ask myself, What is the painter trying to accomplish? What does the painting seem to say? Try looking at a Vincent van Gogh self-portrait the same way he painted it: that is, as though looking into a mirror. Try listening to modern music as though you were sitting beside the composer at the piano.

In music you might start with the *Classical Symphony* by Sergei Prokofiev. Steeped in the music of Joseph Haydn and other Western classical composers, this gifted Russian dashed off this brilliant composition in 1917 while hardly out of the St. Petersburg Conservatory. Move on to listen to his symphonies, operas, and ballets, also his piano and violin concerti. Then enjoy *Peter and the Wolf, The Love for Three Oranges,* and other winsome pieces he wrote about fanciful fairy tales.

Now a classic is the 1913 *Rites of Spring* by Igor Stravinsky. Written for a Paris ballet, it horrified its audience and resulted in an uproar that the police could barely quell. Fifty years later, when I heard it at a concert, I wondered what the fuss was all about. It is truly a watershed piece of music.

Fully alive persons today will want to pay attention to

modern music, as well as to all other things modern, to extend their appreciation as broadly and deeply as possible.

There is no intention here to put modern music above its classic expressions. It is helpful to think of them side by side, neither one superior to the other. In some ways they are the same, but in others they are different. Do not settle for half of a musical loaf, modern or classical. Only the whole loaf of all available music of quality can satisfy the person of mature years.

The person with music solidly lodged within has a constant companion. Stashed away in the recesses of my own memory are, perhaps, a thousand symphonic movements, operatic arias, and string-quartet melodies and themes. Music I have heard over the years is stored away in a disorganized, unintentional fashion. Most of it is subject to recall, although many works pop into my consciousness while I am awake at night or at other odd times when music is not on my mind. It seems to come back to me the way poetry memorized in high school comes back half a century later. As a result, I am never alone; music is my constant companion.

You can also explore the world of classical and modern art. You might start by enrolling in an art course. They are available in most communities. Another way to begin is to read books about art. There are a rich variety complete with illustrations, and in most libraries there are large folio volumes with full-color paintings. A classic treatment of the Impressionists is John Rewald's *History of Impressionism*[1]; equally good is his *Post Impressionism: From van Gogh to Gaugin*[2]. A delightful and enlightening book is *How to Visit a Museum* by David Finn.[3] Equally good for modern art is *The Shock of the New* by Robert Hughes[4]; you may already have read his art columns in *Time* magazine. A fine pamphlet on painting, architecture, and sculpture, *Seeing with the Inner Eye,* can be obtained from AARP's Institute of Lifetime Learning in Washington. Of course, go to museums and galleries whenever you can.

As for books, there are numerous lists of books worth reading. These lists are available in local libraries and through the Library of Congress in Washington. They include modern books as well as classical literature. They can help you fill in the gaps.

A stimulating way to get started with the literature of all time is to read *Classics Revisited* by Kenneth Rexroth.[5] This exhilarating book by a distinguished poet and scholar examines sixty great books of world literature, from the *Epic of Gilgamesh* to *Huckleberry Finn,* and shows how they reflect and illuminate the human condition. To look up every kind of fact and opinion about English literature, there is nothing better than the *Oxford Companion to English Literature,* edited by Margaret Drabble.[6]

What is fascinating about literature and the arts is that they forever change, breaking up and then re-forming. We have to run to keep abreast. Doing so is a stimulating exercise—and a broadening one!

All of us can have a wide range of enjoyment in music, art, and literature, new and old. It is never too late to broaden and deepen our cultural sensitivity, while having a good time doing so. Nor is it too late to travel, both at home and abroad, and thus experience even greater fulfillment. Through travel we can discover many expressions of music, literature, and the arts, to say nothing of scenes of beauty and of historical significance.

Never has it been so easy to see the world! Age is no barrier. Ships and planes go everywhere; only a few countries are forbidden territory.

Although overseas travel is not cheap, there are off-season specials, religious group trips, and nonprofit university course-related tours, all of which are easier on the pocketbook. Elderhostel (see chapter 8) has hundreds of low-cost tours at home and abroad. The cheapest of all travel opportunities are available through the American Youth Hostels. Despite the name, older people are welcome.

Places you have read about all your life are now open and

accessible. Only a few years ago China was largely forbidden territory, but now American tourists are not only welcome but treated with every courtesy. See and climb the Great Wall, visit dozens of magnificent cities, some dating back a thousand years before Christ, come to know a few Chinese, and sail on two of the world's greatest rivers, the Yellow and the Yangtze. While you are so far away from home in East Asia, take time to see Japan with all its beauty and both its historic and modern significance. Be sure to visit nearby Hong Kong, Thailand, Korea, and Taiwan as well.

Somewhat more familiar places include Great Britain, the Soviet Union, Israel and the Arab world, Australia and New Zealand, India, Southern Asia, and South America. Now Eastern Europe is also open to travelers.

While listing all these foreign countries, we should not overlook our own. We seniors could spend the rest of our lives in the United States, seeing its thousands of wonders, natural and man-made. For example, even trying to visit all the U.S. national parks could keep one happily occupied for years.

Whatever your plans, whatever you intend to see in your travels, be sure to prepare adequately in advance and finish with a thorough follow-up upon your return. Read one or more books about the country or countries you will be visiting; it is impossible to know too much about the places you will be seeing.

While you are on the journey, develop "hungry eyes." See everything around you. Drink it all in. Assume you will never be there again, and therefore you must memorize what is before your eyes. Be like blotting paper or a sponge; soak it up. Don't miss a thing. Then review what you have seen as a way of retaining it in your memory. Keep Christopher Morley's statement in mind: "From now on until the end of time no one else will ever see with my eyes, and I mean to make the most of my chance."

When you return home you might want to do an in-depth study of the areas you have visited. Thorough advance preparation and good follow-up will add immeasurably to what you will receive for your time, efforts, and money.

Ralph Waldo Emerson may have had the final word about traveling, reminding us that although we may travel the world over to find the beautiful, if we do not carry it with us we will not find it.

We older men and women are very fortunate in that we have lived long enough to know how to carry the beautiful with us, whether our adventures with travel, music, literature, and art are far-ranging or experienced in the coziness of our favorite chair. Bon voyage!

10
Experience the Rich Life of a Volunteer

Volunteers are invariably happy, fulfilled people. Volunteering gives them a new lift in life. They sense that they are engaged in important concerns. They are paying back to society the debt they owe for their own good life, doing for others what others have done for them earlier in life. They feel good about having the opportunity!

Today's older men and women are likely to be better volunteers than any previous generation. We have a higher and broader level of education, are trained in more skills, are healthier and more adaptable to changing situations, and may be more aware of the vast human needs existing in the world today. It is likely that many of us will have decades to live after reaching the age of sixty and thus will be able to go on contributing year after year.

There is a new flexibility in all of us older folk these days, enabling us to throw off old habits and take up new lives. We can live out our years, not the way others may expect us to but as we ourselves truly want to. It is a new ball game! Or, may we say, it is a new space mission!

Volunteerism has become almost a national industry. In almost every area of life, volunteers have become an essential ingredient. They assist in private and public schools, in libraries, in hospitals and nursing homes, in churches and synagogues, and in community agencies of every kind. Older people living alone and individuals needing a wide range of services receive the thoughtful attention of millions of unsung volunteers. Many people young and old would be the poorer without them.

The statistics for all this are staggering. No complete figures for the nation's volunteers exist. A broad estimate would be that they provide millions of hours of service, worth, at the minimum wage level, billions of dollars. In my small Southwest community of ninety thousand, 802 men and women registered with the Retired Senior Volunteer Program (RSVP) provided 167,400 hours of community assistance in a recent year; at the minimum wage this would total $652,860, or an estimated $6.5 million over a ten-year period. Projected nationwide this amounts to an estimated $80 billion annually. And this estimate does not include the uncounted services given by individual people on their own or through their churches.

The Independent Sector, a Washington-based group representing organizations involved in philanthropy and voluntary activities, reports that churches are a prime source of volunteers. Volunteer activities "by clergy and church members were valued in the study as $13.1 billion. Some 253,000 volunteer clergy gave an average of 70 hours per month, and 10.4 million volunteers other than clergy worked an average of 10 hours per month on congregational [and community] problems."[1]

Furthermore, almost half of all American adults, some 80 million individuals, contribute time to some cause. Most of them give an average of five hours a week, making a total of 19.5 billion hours in 1987. This is the equivalent of 10 million full-time employees.

The American Association of Retired Persons now has more than four hundred thousand volunteers involved in programs related to the aging. These volunteers report that they do so to meet people and to fulfill a sense of duty, but above all because it gives them considerable satisfaction. All senior-citizen membership organizations discovered similar responses.

Even national business organizations are getting into the act. They see the value of voluntarism and strongly support it. They recognize that volunteer activities help fulfill their retirees' lives, as well as being good public relations for the companies. The National Retired Volunteer Center (NRVC) in Minnesota is one such group. Its goal: "To mobilize retirees through their corporations to produce volunteer leadership in their communities." It recognizes retirees as a considerable asset both to their former employers and to their communities. To make voluntarism even more pleasant and productive, NRVC provides help and guidance in specific training activities designed to enrich the retirees' lives while bringing benefits to others.[2]

Of far greater importance than the dollar worth is the human value of the services rendered to millions of individuals every year. They include visits and special services to men and women in jail and prison and to residents of nursing homes and elderly shut-ins, assisting in hospitals and mental institutions, and letter writing for the aged and blind. In education, volunteers tell stories to preschoolers and serve as teachers' aides, tutors, and teachers of functional illiterates. They are also handyman helpers, publicists for agencies, office helpers in volunteer agencies, docents at museums and historic homes, house-builders for Habitat for Humanity, members of special community task forces, tax-aid people, library advisers, swimming teachers for children and older people, translators and interpreters, church school teachers—the list goes on and on.

Some volunteers find their own jobs that need doing. Others are recruited and assigned by churches, synagogues, and service clubs to places of recognized needs. Organizations such as the Retired Senior Volunteer Program compile lists of service requests, which they share and discuss with older people looking for possible assignments.

The need for citizen assistance is clearly growing. With public resources shrinking and society's needs increasing, volunteers are more essential than in any previous time. In every community there are widespread unmet needs. In almost all areas of life, men, women, and children are now suffering because they lack the friendly and skillful help that can come from dedicated volunteers. Our papers report almost daily that public school teachers need more help to lead children into the wider world of knowledge and social skills. This is especially true in run-down neighborhoods where working mothers have little quality time with their children. The phenomenon of working mothers is not limited today to working-class women but has become widespread across the economy. Therefore, serving as teacher's aides may well be one of the most vital contributions to the nation's future that volunteers can make.

Arthur S. Flemming, head of the U.S. Department of Health, Education, and Welfare under President Eisenhower, has pointed out that, while in recent years the nation has trained about 50,000 persons as homemaker/home-health workers, at least 300,000 such skilled persons are needed. Homelessness, now affecting an estimated 3 million people, has a crushing effect upon small children and young people; this condition is found in most communities.

Perhaps a million frail elderly eke out only a bare existence, eventually wasting away from a lack of trained and dedicated care. Even people in nursing homes need friendly visits. Many of them have no family or friends to visit them. They become lonely and withdrawn and consequently lose their everyday living skills and often their essential will to live. At best, the life span of people in nursing homes is often shorter than their physical condition would seem to indicate. In the case of such forgotten and neglected elderly folk, the decline toward death is unnecessarily rapid. Dedicated outside persons—volunteers—can provide essential care to the frail elderly in nursing homes. This should be of top concern to religious groups and their leaders.

A quite unusual opportunity for volunteer service is that of Habitat for Humanity. As with other projects, this one requires dedication and perseverance, plus whatever skills the person has. Habitat recruits volunteers who out of Christian motivation wish to help provide housing for those who can't afford today's market prices. This nonprofit Christian housing ministry works in partnership with people who need to improve their living conditions. Houses are built or renovated, using as much volunteer labor and donated materials as possible. They are then sold to families whose income is too low to secure bank loans through a completely nonprofit, no-interest transaction termed "biblical economics." Building costs are repaid by the family over a fixed period. These payments are recycled to build more houses. Homeowners are required to provide their labor along with the volunteers and also to help later in erecting other Habitat dwellings.[3]

These examples make it evident that you and I can bring about an improvement in the human scene. We may not be able to fashion the whole world closer to our heart's desire, but there are many vital areas of human life where we can make a decided difference.

What is important is to find something we can believe in. It is essential, as an AARP manual points out, to be convinced that what we do is important.

> Once you have defined who you are and what you want to do as a volunteer, the next step is to measure your values. This is not as difficult as it sounds. Look around you and make a list of what bothers you, what troubles you, what upsets you about the world today. Is there too much hunger, too much poverty? . . . Too many children who can't read? . . . Do you worry about older people who are lonely, sick, or victimized? . . . Now look again, is there someone or some group, institution, or agency that is trying to do something to change things for the better? Already you have developed a good understanding not only of what your values are, but also where some good places to volunteer may be.[4]

All around you are institutions and agencies where your volunteer efforts can count for something. Talk to people in the public school administrative office or those you might already know in a neighboring school. Look up "hospice" in the phone book, and investigate the possibilities of the valuable contribution you can make through this ministry to persons who are terminally ill. Hospitals always have important volunteer jobs to fill. RSVP will have a long list of nearby community jobs to be tackled. The area American Red Cross chapter will have suggestions. Your local AARP chapter may be looking for people to work in its tax-assistance program. Talk to people in your local political party office about where you might fit in. For ideas, visit social agencies and senior citizen centers near you, and don't forget Planned Parenthood. Consider a role in the peace and environment groups in your community. Your church or synagogue will surely have ideas and suggestions as to where you might serve people in need. At the same time, you are assisting your religious institution to reach out into the community.

In many cases the job will require no special training. For example, no qualifications other than goodwill and faithfulness are needed to buy groceries or pay bills for shut-ins. Many important tasks, however, require simple or even more extended technical training. Volunteers will welcome the opportunity to receive special orientation and training. Everything we learn expands our minds and leads to our further growth. Remember the old saying: It is never too late to learn. Look on additional training as an indication that you are worth training!

If you are seriously considering serving as a volunteer, you will need to look again at the meaning of the word "work." Volunteering, if taken seriously, is work in its full spiritual and psychological sense. For some people work is a terrible drudge, something to avoid if possible and to escape as soon as feasible. Others, however, live fully only through their work. It gives their life meaning. In their work activities they are challenged to take on new responsibilities, which lead to additional achievement and satisfaction. It is through one's working life that much human character is formed. Work, whether for pay or for satisfaction while volunteering, bestows a certain dignity and quality. Our Creator has built into us the need to work. In our work we are sharing in God's creative activity.

As Howard Shank wrote in *Managing Retirement,* one's working career can become synonymous with life itself. "It is not just a livelihood. It is a sport, pastime, hobby, lover. It provides our friends and our social life. It sets our goals, defines our ambitions, gives us our report cards. Slowly, seductively, it comes to define the very word 'important.' "[5] And as Dr. Paul Pruyser of the Menninger Foundation has affirmed, "If loving and working are pillars of health maintenance, as Freud says, the reduction of work undermines the very structure of personality."[6]

The message then is clear: NEVER RETIRE! While at age sixty-five or earlier you may end a long-term relationship with a company or profession, quickly continue your work experience in a solid volunteer assignment, in going back to school, or in a part-time job—or all three! As Howard Shank advises, "Work for the good of your self-esteem. Work for the fun of working. . . . Work to satisfy your survival instincts and your work ethic." That is, retire from your particular job or occupation, but not from life, not from work, not from involvement.[7]

A saying attributed to Ben Franklin puts it very cleverly: There is nothing wrong with retirement so long as it does not interfere with your work!

When a goal-oriented man or woman retires, this person is likely to maintain a similar orientation to life, although perhaps with a quite different set of goals. Serving as a volunteer then not only makes a valuable contribution to the community but also sustains and strengthens the inner spirit that keeps people going through coming decades. Volunteer work helps guarantee continued spiritual health.

11

Be Out of Step as Much as Possible

The world owes a debt of gratitude to its critics, dissidents, nonconformists, and agitators. As far back as recorded history takes us, we find men and women who broke out of the accepted mold and took giant steps toward creating a better life for humankind.

Today's world, though often troublesome, would be infinitely worse if there had not been rebels who made a sharp break with society's accepted patterns and stood boldly for genuine solutions to humanity's problems.

Through our seniority you and I have earned the right to look critically at today's world. We have also been given the responsibility to call the attention of our country to situations and conditions that need drastic improvement. It has been said that much is required of those to whom much is given. So it should be with us.

Older folks today make up what might be called the "far-too-long-silent generation." Seldom have we stood up for our rights, which were earned over a lifetime of working and giving and sharing, nor have we been critics of a society in which others suffer from inequality and lack of opportunity. Our sizable minority of 30 million is far too unprotesting and acquiescent. Rather than becoming the powerful moral and political force we could be, we have, for the most part, remained silent spectators of what was going on around us.

One does not need to be a perfectionist to recognize large areas of American life needing solid improvement. It is not that life in our blessed country is not good, but that with its historic ideals and its enormous potential it should be better.

We of the older generation could legitimately complain about our largely unrecognized status. However, we should first stand up for concerns of other people. We would be less than genuinely mature if the only rights we defended were our own. Today, after a lifetime of thinking about our own problems, we can move beyond ourselves into areas where other human beings enjoy life far less than we do. This country has more than enough individuals and groups who speak only for themselves.

Adequate food, shelter, and medical care for all people is of first importance. Even in the richest nation in the world, millions of our people lack these absolute necessities of life. The Center on Budget and Policy Priorities indicates that in spite of U.S. economic recovery, poverty continues to increase, especially among American minorities. Eight million more persons now live in poverty than in 1978, a total of 32.5 million. Children are especially vulnerable. One fifth of all children under eighteen years of age live in poverty, the worst record among industrial nations. The average income of a family in poverty is $4,165, which after adjustment for inflation is the lowest since 1959, when such statistical data was first compiled. An estimated 3 million people in America are homeless. Many of them are elderly couples or families with young children who find shelter in cars, tents, or abandoned buildings. According to the Select Committee on Aging of the House of Representatives, "Thirty percent of the elderly live in substandard, deteriorating, or dilapidated housing."[1] Thirty-seven million Americans lack adequate medical insurance coverage. In the area of infant mortality the United States ranks twenty-second among the nations, similar to the ranking of some Third World countries.[2]

Why many of these conditions exist is suggested in recent releases by two Washington think tanks as reported in the *Christian Science Monitor* in an article on the growing income gap in this country. According to the Economic Policy Institute, "The economy of the 1980s left most workers worse off, while 1 percent enjoyed a windfall; latest statistics reveal that working Americans have experienced declining real wages, decreasing living standards and worsening income inequality throughout the 1980s." The Center on Budget and Policy Priorities reports, "The richest 1 percent of all Americans now receive nearly as much income after taxes as the bottom 40 percent of Americans combined. Stated another way, the richest 2.5 million people now have nearly as much income as the 100 million Americans with the lowest income. Furthermore, the share of national income going to those in the middle of the income scale is now lower than at any time since the end of World War II."[3]

Is it not proper for older people to consider themselves out of step with a society largely indifferent to this human tragedy?

Universal quality education is another necessity in the kind of world in which we live. Public school education has been slowly deteriorating for some years. When we read about Japanese education, we realize that we are way behind in scholastic achievement. For groups such as Hispanic and black children education is even less adequate, especially in the inner cities. More Hispanics and blacks are dropping out of high school before graduation than at any other time. Today's dropouts make up 25 percent of the total school population, with 40 percent of blacks and over 50 percent of Hispanics dropping out.[4]

This situation is an example of poor national priorities. If our rich and powerful nation is to remain that way, it must provide the finest and most complete schooling for all its children. It is not difficult for older people to be somewhat out of step with our present educational system.

Any country genuinely concerned about future generations would care about the problems of the damaged environment and rising population, in our own country and in the world. In these areas we are not doing even passably well.

Acid rain is slowly killing our lakes and streams, fish and forests. Hazardous nuclear waste dumps threaten to contaminate drinking water in many areas. Nuclear-plant air pollution kills both human beings and animals. Even the oceans are becoming polluted from out-of-control dumping. If present tree cutting continues, almost half the world's forests will be gone within fifteen years. Deserts are spreading in many parts of the globe.[5]

Scientists warn us that auto exhaust fumes and factory smokestack emissions are affecting the sun's rays. The greenhouse effect caused by pollution could one day melt the arctic ice and cause disastrous flooding of seaports, with the corresponding loss of cities and living areas. The warming of the earth could sharply reduce the production of food, here and around the world.[6]

A mid-1990 United Nations report, the result of the combined expertise of a thousand scientists around the world, concluded that global warming has already begun. This warning poses serious threats to the planet, including rising sea levels, the spread of disease, and mass starvation in poor countries. In the next century, temperatures will rise faster than in the last ten thousand years. Curbing greenhouse gases requires immediate and urgent measures, the UN report said.[7]

A less familiar danger is the serious loss of ozone in the outer atmosphere. This could mean the intensification of the sun's rays, with disastrous effects both on human skin and on the fertility of the land. The sun, now a friendly source of light and heat, could one day become our enemy. Already the ozone depletion area over the South Pole is as large as the continental United States. This is caused by the release into the atmosphere of chlorofluorocarbons (CFCs). This gas is used in refrigerators, air conditioners, spray cans, and other products. Very little is being done to prevent this staggering disaster.

In addition, paving over, building, erosion, and other misuses of our finest soil are reducing America's arable land.

Every year the increasing loss of farmland forces more people to move to our already overcrowded cities. One day this country could be soil poor, just as eventually it could be forest poor.[8]

As the Population Institute has pointed out, "We live in a world of more than five billion people, which grew last year by an unprecedented 90 million. Three billion young people will enter their reproductive years within this generation."[9] We are peopling our world to eventual death. Overpopulation inevitably brings on war and aggression as well as starvation, as is true of sections of Africa today. The whole world, including the United States, is producing new human begins faster than essential food supplies.

Two hundred years ago, Thomas Malthus predicted that human births would soon exceed the ability of agriculture to produce enough food for everyone. Wars and famine would then emerge to keep the population at a sustainable level. Over the years his views were ridiculed. Only in our day is his forecast coming true.

When they become aware of these painful predictions, mature people must oppose the complacency of the majority on these life-and-death issues. They will wish to be part of the alert minority who refuse to continue in an unthinking lockstep, preferring to strike out on their own.

Our country's trade deficit and the staggering national debt continue to weaken our economy. Many objective observers feel that the United States is losing its competitive edge in the world's markets. Internal and overseas indebtedness is using up funds that otherwise could be used to strengthen our schools and raise the standard of living of the poor and unemployed.

Much of America's financial problem is due to its three-hundred-billion-dollar defense budget. These expenditures use up funds taken from a wide variety of civilian needs. Child care, the schools, the elderly, and medical care for all Americans suffer because of inadequate funding. Many questions have been raised concerning the shortsightedness of this country in defining national security solely in military terms. The United States is not secure as long as basic human needs go unmet.[10]

Recently the General Accounting Office documented the deterioration of the nation's infrastructure. To renovate our bridges and interstate highways would require $500 billion. The GAO stated further that $20 billion would be needed for low-cost housing, $150 billion to clean up toxic waste, and more than $100 billion to free nuclear weapons plants from existing contamination.[11]

Of primary concern to everyone is the curse of drug addiction, which is reaching every level of American life, even touching young children. The spread of addiction raises serious questions as to the character and inner motivation of the people of this country. What can be wrong with people who engage in this deliberate act of self-destruction? This sickness goes beyond anything laws can cure. This is of great social and spiritual concern.

We are now forced to conclude that what has been happening to us and the world is not the result of an act of God or the operation of fate. What has taken place is clearly the result of human planning and design—or at least the unfortunate outcome of our expanding industrial economy.

The human race is mortgaging its own future.

To be out of step in all these important matters is not to be negative. Supreme Court Justice Oliver Wendell Holmes was called "The Great Dissenter." But as Catherine Drinker Bowen points out in *Yankee from Olympus*, "The title was misleading. 'To want something fiercely and want it all the time'—this is not dissent but affirmation. The things Holmes wanted were great things, never to be realized. How can man realize the infinite? 'Have faith and pursue the infinite.' "[12]

Eminent lawyer William Stringfellow stood up positively for his convictions in the 1960s. Immediately upon graduating from Harvard Law School he, a white man, moved into a 12-by-25-foot apartment in one of the worst slum areas of black Harlem. (A family of eight had lived there previously.) He went there, he said, as a lawyer and to serve as a layperson in the local Episcopal church.

He felt compelled as a Christian to identify, if only at a superficial level, with people suffering the sad lot of the underclass. They were enduring deadening poverty, squalor, poor housing, bad smells, second-class jobs or no jobs at all, widespread discrimination, frustration.

Out of this experience came a remarkable little book, *My People Is the Enemy*. In it he expressed the "terrible premonition I suffer about what lies ahead for all Americans in the harsh days which shall come upon the nation in the crisis of their land." He was stunned by "the hostility between the rich and the poor, and the alienation between the races."[13]

Not many of us will be able to do what he did—or think we should—but he was an example of a modern man deliberately out of step with conventional society. He acted out of an overwhelming conviction that only brotherhood and racial harmony could save the nation.

Older people cannot go along complacently in today's world, because they have positive convictions as to what their society should be. These are not utopian dreams. They are matters that could be set right if only they were considered top priorities by those who make the nation's decisions. Events of recent years would indicate that basic human issues have not been included on our country's agenda. By calling for a change in the nation's priorities, the older segment of the population could help counteract the present imbalance. It is time to exert a positive influence—in local government, in state capitals, and in Washington.

What is essential is that people with convictions make a public stand based on their convictions. It is time for you and me to become advocates, activists, people who take stands on vital matters. We might appear negative and critical, but our protests arise from a positive belief that this nation must fulfill its noble promise. Over the centuries this country has been a beacon to the world. May it now, with the support of the older generation, become a land of plenty for all, with peace between all groups and races, justice for everyone, and a renewed vision of America's innate greatness.

This is central to what it means to be an older man or woman in the 1990s. To be mature, we need to act responsibly in both our personal lives and in the larger world. We must be willing to be out of step when we cannot do otherwise and still retain our self-respect.

12

Be Ever the Advocate

Involved and responsible persons cannot look with complacency on today's world. There is too wide a gulf between what is and what ought to be for us to sit back comfortably and accept the status quo. Society as a whole and individuals in it are suffering immeasurably.

The potential power of one person to make a difference is beyond our imagining. Great historic movements have started when one man or one woman became convinced that certain situations and conditions demanded change and improvement. Many communities got libraries, colleges, and hospitals because one person cared enough to start something. We have the examples of Emmaline Pankhurst in England and Elizabeth Cady Stanton and Susan B. Anthony in the United States, who fought for the vote and other rights for women. In New England, Wendell Phillips and others set in motion the movement to abolish human slavery.

More recently, Martin Luther King, Jr., brought about significant changes in human understanding and practice. He never held elective office, and at the outset he was very hesitant about taking any action that would appear to be political. As events moved on, however, he saw that he and his movement would have to enter the political arena.

We people of mature years are not Martin Luther Kings, nor is it our job to organize public demonstrations. Nevertheless, we can use our respected position in society to help push our country in the direction of more fundamental humaneness, decency, and equality. To do so demands taking stands, becoming political.

There is much that you and I can do toward this end. Wringing our hands in despair must be but a brief prelude to taking strong positions on what can and should be done about the human condition. We older persons are obligated to devote our energies toward wiping out the injustices we deplore. Our righteous indignation should be backed by an intelligent analysis of the situation. This, in turn, should lead us to identify ourselves with organizations and forces offering positive and creative alternatives to what we consider wrong and harmful. The world and our own integrity demand our involvement. In short, we should be advocates.

What is an advocate? What does it mean to be an advocate? To be an advocate is to be a volunteer, but a volunteer plus!

A volunteer gives time and concern to help existing organizations fulfill their humane and uplifting aims and goals. The volunteer fits into their aims and purposes. In contrast, an advocate seeks to create new means for human betterment, to find fresh approaches to old issues and problems, to espouse new causes designed to transform society.

A volunteer helps and supports individuals needing every kind of assistance. The advocate investigates new ways to eliminate the age-old curses of war, hunger, homelessness, and racial and class conflicts.

The volunteer fits into the normal scheme of things, using dedication and goodwill to bring about improvement in the status quo. The advocate seeks to create more fundamental and long-lasting solutions to today's distressful situations.

The volunteer seeks to assist humanity within present social structures. The advocate would create fresh structures to confront ancient evils in their contemporary expressions.

The volunteer brings a human touch to people suffering from pain, hunger, trouble, and sorrow. The advocate seeks to eliminate the basic causes of these ills.

The volunteer thinks of charity, relief, and material assistance, either given directly to individuals or through agencies. The advocate acts upon the belief that establishing unlimited justice and total equality will eliminate the root causes of human distress.

The two approaches complement each other. The volunteer seeks to utilize and improve the best of today's society, while the advocate seeks a reconstructed society dedicated to serving human needs.

The volunteer is absolutely essential to the continued function and workability of present-day society. The advocate envisions a better world for tomorrow and seeks to bring it into being. Society cannot thrive with only one or the other, but requires both for completion and perfection.

A problem arises when we propose that people of mature views become advocates for a better way of life for all. There are no parties one can join to work to these ends. In some Western countries, notably those in Scandinavia, minority third-party political groups offer detailed programs of social and economic change. This is not true in the United States today.

This country has, however, a rich abundance of voluntary organizations offering programs and proposals touching all the areas of American life needing constructive change. You will find at the end of the chapter some information about groups working in the following areas of concern.

Poverty. In the face of the widespread poverty and hunger and homelessness in this richest nation in the world, many groups support programs seeking a fairer and more equitable distribution of life's necessities to everyone. Children of the world should share in our concern and our largess.

Budget priorities. Our federal budget should give top priority to the vast array of needs of men, women, and children within our civilian economy. The federal government must take the lead in switching priorities from guns to plowshares, investing in research and training of personnel for the civilian economy, and funding the repair of the neglected national infrastructure. This will be possible when military expenditures reflect the new world situation of the 1990s rather than the Cold War fears of previous decades.

Economic conversion. The present military-dominated economy can be converted into one that gives priority to social and national needs. The emphasis here is upon economic diversification and expansion that could eventually both satisfy domestic consumer needs and provide challenging products for export.

Population policy. We need a rational and balanced population policy at home and abroad. Our national resources can be used to assist Third World countries facing a staggering out-of-control population growth.

Environment. There is need to urge strong national concern and immediate action favoring the environment, both in this country and around the world. If we continue to destroy natural resources, we condemn future generations to a second- or third-rate level of existence.

Education. Far better schools are needed so that in America's next century there will be sufficiently well-educated and technically trained young people to compete in the world. Schools should be sufficiently attractive to reduce the current disastrous dropout rate at both elementary and high school levels.

Medical care. Adequate medical care should be available to all Americans. Legislation concerning universal medical care must be passed and put into effect.

National priorities. During the Cold War, the nation thought it prudent to subordinate certain domestic programs and budget items to what was considered to be military necessity. With a new worldview at hand and military budgets being cut, it is essential that the nation as a whole review its priorities. Included would be a concern about reducing our dependence on foreign oil. This can mean increased budget support for the important concerns listed above. Even more important in the end, this could be a broad review of national aims and purposes in light of today's burgeoning needs and our fundamental historical ideals.

The national office of your church or synagogue also has information about these issues. Religious bodies make yearly statements on important matters and seek to educate their members concerning them. Your local religious leader may be able to supply some of these materials to you.

Religious publications that come to your home may have articles on these subjects. Nondenominational publications such as *The Christian Century*[1] and *Christianity and Crisis*,[2] available in some libraries, will give you perspective on these issues. In your public library, look at journals of opinion such as *The Nation*[3] for a different kind of coverage. Some of these publications are quite unorthodox, but they are stimulating and educational.

Contact your state and federal senators and representatives. Ask them for information about government publications on the subjects of your interest. Urge them to introduce legislation that will help our country to be more humane, more caring, more dedicated to solid solutions to the problems that concern you.

Explore your community library. Talk with the librarian about books on the subjects outlined earlier. Some libraries will have organized study groups on these issues. Help to organize one or more groups if they do not already exist.

Your local college or university will have scholars and teachers informed about hunger, disarmament, population issues, and related matters. Ask these people for information and guidance. Perhaps regular or special courses along the line of your subjects of inquiry are already offered.

Inquire around your community and within your circle of friends. It is likely that there are groups already looking into some of the matters that concern you. Perhaps you can bring together like-minded people for discussion. Organizations such as the Foreign Policy Association provide study guides for your use.[4]

Intelligent and concerned older people will want to consider the political realities affecting everything in society. Then, within the range of their powers and influence, they can seek to strengthen the forces within our nation that stand for peace, justice, and brotherhood. To be advocates for a world closer to the heart's desire is a responsibility just made for people of mature judgment and advanced years.

Suggested References

Poverty

American Friends Service Committee, 1501 Cherry Street, Philadelphia, PA 19102

Catholic Relief Services, 1101 1st Avenue, New York, NY 10022

Division of Church World Service, 475 Riverside Drive, Room 678, New York, NY 10115

Educators for Social Responsibility, 23 Garden Street, Cambridge, MA 02138

Food First (Institute for Food and Development Policy), 145 Ninth Street, San Francisco, CA 94103

Institute for Public Affairs, 2040 N. Milwaukee Avenue, Chicago, IL 60647

Budget Priorities

American Association of University Women, 240 Virginia Avenue, NW, Washington, DC 20037

Better World Society, 1100 17th Street, NW, Washington, DC, 20036

Council on Economic Priorities, 30 Irving Place, New York, NY 10003

Friends Committee on National Legislation, 245 Second Street, NE, Washington, DC 20002

League of Women Voters, 1730 M Street, NE, Washington, DC 10036

Physicians for Social Responsibility, 1000 16th Street, SW, Washington, DC 20036

Economic Conversion

Center for Economic Conversion, 222C View Street, Mountain View, CA 94041

Council on Economic Priorities, 30 Irving Place, New York, NY 10003

Friends Committee on National Legislation, 245 Second Street, NE, Washington, DC 20002

Physicians for Social Responsibility, 1000 16th Street, SW, Washington, DC 20036

SANE/FREEZE, 1819 H Street, NW, Washington, DC 20006

Population Policy

Alan Guttmacher Institute, 115 Fifth Avenue, New York, NY 10003

National Abortion Rights Action League (NARAL), 1101 14th Street, NW, Washington, DC 20005

Planned Parenthood Federation, 810 Seventh Avenue, New York, NY 10019

Population Institute, 110 Maryland Avenue, NE, Suite 207, Washington, DC 20002

Zero Population Growth, 1400 16th Street, NW, Washington, DC 20036

Environment

Earthwatch, 680 Mt. Auburn Street, Box 403, Watertown, MA 02172

Environmental Defense Fund, 257 Park Avenue South, New York, NY 10010

Global Education Associates, 475 Riverside Drive, New York, NY 10115

Greenpeace, 1436 U Street, NW, Washington, DC 20009

National Audubon Society, 950 Third Avenue, New York, NY 10022

National Resources Defense Council, 40 West 20th Street, New York, NY 10168

Sierra Club, 730 Polk Street, San Francisco, CA 94109

Education

Better World Society, 1100 17th Street, NW, Washington, DC 20036

Educators for Social Responsibility, 23 Garden Street, Cambridge, MA 02138

Friends Committee on National Legislation, 245 Second Street, NE, Washington, DC 20002

National Education Association, 1201 16th Street, NW, Washington, DC 20005

National Priorities

Council on Economic Priorities, 30 Irving Place, New York, NY 10003

Common Cause, 2030 M Street, NW, Washington, DC 20036

Fellowship of Reconciliation, Box 271, Nyack, NY 10960

Friends Committee on National Legislation, 245 Second Street, NE, Washington, DC 20002

Your Senators and Representatives

Epilogue: Make Your Life a Work of Art

The field of the creative arts offers new and wonderful opportunities to older people. Those who engage in these artistic pursuits gain a new confidence in themselves, a conviction that their advanced years have not put them on the shelf. Life at its best is creative, and an ever larger group of older people is discovering this truth.

Have you thought of using your instincts and talents on yourself? Not only paintings and pottery are works of art and expressions of our human talent for creativity. You and I can also become works of art. We ourselves are the artists and creators. This creation needs neither oils nor watercolors, neither canvas nor potter's clay. It needs only the experience of living which we older people have in abundance.

Of course, creating or re-creating ourselves is not as easy as using a paintbrush or throwing a pot. Our common humanity is often more resistant than the clay one molds by hand. Anyone seeking to remake himself or herself must realize that self-creation is an even more rigorous exercise than learning to paint with oils or using the chisel and hammer on marble.

The search for our personal fulfillment as human beings takes us into three areas: body, mind, and spirit. Each is a separate entity, but each counts only when linked to the others.

Body. Body suggests physical health, keeping the body as active and fine-tuned as is possible at one's age. Rare is the creative person whose physical being is in disrepair. Men and women at their best find themselves described by the old saying: A sound mind in a sound body.

Some of us are blessed with healthy, fully functioning bodies; others are not. What counts usually is what we do with what we have. The champion golfer is not born that way but, through great effort and amazing determination, achieves the skills he or she displays. So we can care for, develop, and use whatever physical strength and ability we may have.

We do not know exactly what Paul meant when he said, "I keep under my body, and bring it into subjection" (1 Cor. 9:27, KJV). Surely he must have meant that he kept his body under control, rather than allowing his body and its appetites to control him. He emphasized the important role of the body when he wrote, "Your body is a temple of the Holy Spirit within you" (1 Cor. 6:19). The other two elements of the triad, mind and spirit, cannot function fully if we neglect or abuse their housing, the body.

Mind. Mind encompasses far more than the "brain" with which mind is often confused. The sixteenth-century poet Sir Edward Dyer had the right conception of the richness of the mind when he wrote, "My mind to me a kingdom is." There is nothing known to us as magnificent as the human mind. It is the seat of genuine knowledge, of choice and decision, the motivating power behind our lives. The mind at work has filled our world and our lives with whatever glory they possess.

Four centuries ago, England's tight little island kingdom may have been for Sir Edward Dyer a worthy comparison for the human mind. Now we see that the mind is more like a universe than a kingdom, a compact, invisible universe inside the human being. It is to the total living person what the heart is to the body and brain. It is the nondictatorial executive, determining everything we are and all we do. We may marvel at the latest super-computer, but the mind makes this pale into insignificance. The mind is the original computer. It not only solves problems but remembers and recalls, all without any buttons to push or systems to learn. It is always on ready.

Webster's *New Universal Unabridged Dictionary* describes the mind as the seat of thinking, perception, feeling, and willing, the center of the individual's consciousness, intellect, or intelligence, and the sum of all conscious and unconscious experiences.

There is no quick fix for an undeveloped mind. It is not like the brain, which may be packed full of facts by memorizing the *Encyclopedia Britannica*. It grows as a product of experience, of making choices and decisions, of living among human beings and coming to terms with them. It grows through inquisitiveness and experimentation. It is fed by love and struggle, by victory and defeat, by fighting against the twin perils of poverty and riches. No pat formula enlarges it, but everything in life adds to it.

The mind can be expanded by exposure to the world's great music, art, and literature. It can develop in dedicated volunteer work, or through experimenting with art and writing, or by giving generously to victims of famine, discrimination, and civil strife, or by putting one's own life and presence on the line when important human issues are at stake. The mind will enlarge itself, given enough exposure to all of life.

Paul referred often to the mind as that which significantly affects the whole person. For example, he wrote, "Let this mind be in you, which was also in Christ Jesus" (Phil. 2:5, KJV).

Spirit. As for spirit, almost everyone agrees that in life there is a spiritual dimension. Most people sense there is something above and beyond the physical body and brain. As far back as history takes us, men and women have experienced the existence of a power not their own that influenced them. Many people call this power God; some sensitive souls have used such terms as the Holy, the Great

Father, the Universal Spirit, the Other, and the Mysterium Tremendum.

Ways by which the spirit in one's life can be developed and increased are varied. Most people experience spiritual growth through participation in public corporate worship and regular private devotions. However, the spiritual is found more in what we are than in what we do, more in our life of faithfulness and dedication than in our religious practices.

The spiritual dimension of life is so essential to us that we can well afford to consider our involvement with it as equal in importance to anything else we do about improving our bodies or minds. In fact, spirit is even more important, for it gives quality and significance to everything we do and all we are. The spiritual is not just one more aspect of human life; rather, it is the essence, the central core of our being. It infuses all of life.

How you and I put all these facets of life together is what really counts. Our highest desires, our most fervent hopes, our noblest visions, our sincerest prayers, our most determined efforts—all these lift us above the common level of existence to a life of higher purpose and achievement. This elevated state of life is well within the reach of all of us. In the end, we are what we make of ourselves.

The December, 1986, round-the-world flight of *Voyager* caught the imagination of everyone. What was amazing was that *Voyager* somewhat resembles the 1903 Wright brothers' plane. It, too, is a kind of homemade do-it-yourself flying machine which obviously couldn't fly, but did! A few dedicated souls worked for years on *Voyager,* figuring out its aerodynamics and building its nonmetallic wings and body, layer by layer. Finally two of the plane's makers, Jeana Yeager and Dick Rutan, flew it successfully around the world without stopping for fuel.

We older people should take to heart a lesson from this feat. It is not that you or I should design a new airplane and fly it. But we can learn something from the hard work, courage, adaptability, ingenuity, and persistence that went into the plane and its flight. These characteristics are essential in the creation by older men and women of their new high-flying years of mature enjoyment.

When we were born into this world there was struggle and pain on the part of our mothers, and we were pushed out of the safe haven of the womb into a strange world. This experience is not unlike what many persons of retirement age face as their customary life changes. It is a time to remember the builders and pilots of *Voyager*. The journey will be different, but the effort and imaginative adaptation required are similar. In this respect, a worthwhile life before and after sixty requires just about the same qualities.

As we look over our lives at this point in our long journey, we are alive in a sense of far greater significance than mere physical survival. We are exploring all of life's possibilities, engaging in fresh enterprises, concerning ourselves with a broad array of important matters. Perhaps we are more truly alive than in any of our earlier decades!

We see ourselves as whole persons—physically, mentally, socially, artistically. Many of us are more healthy in body, mind, and spirit than in previous years. We are fulfilling our earlier promise as human beings created in the image of God. We are living up to the limit of our potentialities, often for the first time in our lives. We see a rich future ahead of us. We understand now that the growing process never ends for the creative person.

One day history will record that, in the late twentieth century, older people broke out of the earlier rigid mold of conventional aging and demonstrated by their adventurous new spirit and outlook what the full span of human life was destined to be—lived to the end in full, magnificent stature.

Notes

Introduction

1. See Jerry Gerber, Janet Wolf, Walter Klores, and Gene Brown, *Lifetrends: The Future of Baby Boomers and Other Aging Americans* (New York: Macmillan Publishing Co., 1990).

2. Howard P. Chudacoff, *How Old Are You?* (Princeton, N.J.: Princeton University Press, 1989).

3. The National Institute on Aging estimates that there are four million patients with Alzheimer's Disease and related mental disorders (The *News* of the Select Committee on Aging of the U.S. House of Representatives, May 10, 1989). There are an estimated three million others who are in nursing homes, bedridden at home, blind, or suffering a crippling ailment. It is very difficult to tally the many unknown men and women who are not in institutions but live alone or with their families. On the other hand, many people with arthritis and other ailments are able to live normal lives.

Chapter 1: Welcome to a Wider World

1. Erich Fromm, *For the Love of Life* (New York: Free Press, 1986), p. 6.

2. Simone de Beauvoir, *Coming of Age* (New York: G.P. Putnam's Sons, 1972), p. 540.

3. Jerry Gerber, Janet Wolf, Walter Klores, and Gene Brown, *Lifetrends: The Future of Baby Boomers and Other Aging Americans* (New York: Macmillan Publishing Co., 1990).

Chapter 2: Explore Your Inner Self

1. Abraham H. Maslow, *Self-Esteem, Self-Actualization* (Monterey, Calif.: Brooks-Cole Publishing Co., 1973). The chapter is a summary of pp. 162–200.
2. Ibid., p. 162.
3. Ibid., p. 196.
4. George Leonard, *Esquire,* December 1983.

Chapter 3: Never Give In—Never, Never, Never

1. Quoted in *New York Times Book Review,* April 19, 1987, p. 47.
2. Judith Thurman, *Isak Dinesen* (New York: St. Martin's Press, 1982), p. 346.
3. "A Song for Occupations," in Mark Van Doren, ed., *The Portable Walt Whitman* (New York: Viking Press, 1945), pp. 102, 107; lines 82, 83, 87, 92, 94, 168.

Chapter 4: Be Proud of Your Age

1. Walter J. Levy and Helen L. West, "Knowledge of Aging Among Clergy," *Journal of Religion and Aging.* vol. 32, no. 3/4, 1989.

Chapter 6: Sex, Sexuality, Sensuality, Love

1. Robert N. Butler with Myra I. Lewis, *Sex After Sixty: A Guide for Men and Women for Their Later Years* (New York: Harper & Row, 1976), pp. 8–9.
2. Doris B. Hammond, *My Parents Never Had Sex* (Buffalo, N.Y.: Prometheus Books, 1988).
3. William H. Masters and Virginia E. Johnson, *Human Sexual Response* (Boston: Little, Brown & Co., 1976), pp. 223, 243–244, 251–252.
4. George Leonard, *Esquire,* December 1982.
5. American Association of Retired Persons, *Aging America* (pamphlet), Washington, D.C., 1985–86.
6. The Commonwealth Fund Commission, "Aging Alone," New York, 1988.
7. Butler, *Sex After Sixty,* p. 141.
8. Ibid., pp. 144–145.

Chapter 7: Expand Your Spiritual Well-being

1. Carl G. Jung, *Modern Man in Search of a Soul* (New York: Harcourt, Brace & Co., 1933), p. 229.
2. Roy W. Fairchild, *Princeton Seminary Bulletin*. Princeton Theological Seminary, New Series, 1987.
3. Notice, exhibit, Millicent Rogers Museum, Taos, New Mexico.
4. Shirley MacLaine, *Out on a Limb* (New York: Bantam Books, 1983).
5. Quoted in "The Aging Connection," American Society on Aging, San Francisco, May–June 1986.
6. National Interfaith Coalition on Aging, Athens, Georgia. Issued in sheet form by the American Association of Retired Persons, Washington, D.C., NICA copyright 1975.
7. Quoted in Henry Goddard Leach (arranger), *Living Philosophies* (New York: Simon & Schuster, 1931), pp. 6, 7.
8. Alfred, Lord Tennyson, *In Memoriam*, book 1.
9. Quoted by Malcolm Cowley, *The View from Eighty* (New York: Viking Press, 1980), pp. 57–58.
10. Edna St. Vincent Millay, "God's World," in *Collected Poems*, (New York: Harper & Row, 1981).

Chapter 8: Stretch Your Mind to the Limit

1. R. H. Moody, "Generations," American Society on Aging, San Francisco, 1987–88, p. 6.
2. For further information, write Elderhostel, 80 Boylston Street, Boston, MA 02116, for a free detailed catalog giving costs, places, courses, schedules, and tours.
3. K. Warner Schaie and G. Labourie, *Life-Span Development Psychology* (New York: Academic Press, 1973), pp. 91–92.
4. Ken Dychtwald and Joe Flower, *Age Wave* (Los Angeles: Jeremy P. Tarcher, 1989), p. 156.

Chapter 9: Seek to Broaden Your World

1. John Rewald, *History of Impressionism,* rev. ed. (New York: Museum of Modern Art, 1969).

2. Ibid., *Post Impressionism: From van Gogh to Gaugin* (New York: Museum of Modern Art, 1962).

3. David Finn, *How to Visit a Museum* (New York: Harry N. Abrams, 1985).

4. Robert Hughes, *The Shock of the New* (New York: Alfred A. Knopf, 1981).

5. Kenneth Rexroth, *Classics Revisited* (Chicago: Quadrangle Books, 1968).

6. Margaret Drabble, ed., *Oxford Companion to English Literature* (New York: Oxford University Press, 5th ed., 1985).

Chapter 10: Experience the Rich Life of a Volunteer

1. Independent Sector, 1828 L Street, NW, Washington, D.C., 20036.

2. National Council on Aging, Washington, D.C., "Perspective on Aging," Nov.–Dec. 1988.

3. Habitat for Humanity, 491 West Church Street, Americus, GA 31709.

4. American Association of Retired Persons, "To Serve, Not to Be Served," AARP Guide, 1983, p. 11.

5. Howard Shank, *Managing Retirement* (Chicago: Contemporary Books, 1985), p. 12.

6. Quoted by Shank, op. cit., p. 17.

7. Ibid., page 17.

Chapter 11: Keep Out of Step as Much as Possible

1. *Section 202: Housing Budget Crisis*, November 1988, U.S. Government Printing Office, Washington, DC, 20202.

2. Publications of the Center on Budget and Policy Priorities (777 North Capitol Street, NE, Washington, DC 20002):

"Holes in the Safety Net: Poverty Programs in the States"

"The Decreasing Anti-Poverty Effectiveness of Government Benefit Programs"

"Falling Through the Safety Net: Latinos and the Declining Effectiveness of Anti-Poverty Programs"

"Smaller Slices of the Pie: The Growing Economic Vulnerability of Poor and Moderate Income Americans"

"The Rural Disadvantage: Growing Income Disparities Between Rural and Urban Areas"

"Poverty in Rural America: A National Overview"

"Laboring For Less: Working But Poor in Rural America"

"Making Work Pay: A New Agenda for Poverty Policies"

"Ending Poverty," *State of the World 1990,* Norton, NY 10110, 1990, pp. 135–153.

"Building an American Health System," Select Committee on Aging, House of Representatives, Washington, DC 20002.

3. *Christian Science Monitor,* September 4, 1990, p. 6.

4. Educators for Social Responsibility, 23 Garden Street, Cambridge, MA 02138; Better World Society, 1100 17th Street, NW, Washington, DC 20036; Friends Committee on National Legislation, 245 Second Street, NE, Washington, DC 20002.

5. Sierra Club, 730 Polk Street, San Francisco, CA 94109. *State of the World 1990,* op. cit. National Resources Defense Council, 40 West 20th Street, New York, NY 10168. Zero Population Growth, 1400 16th Street, NW, Washington, DC 20036. Bill McKibbon, *The End of Nature* (New York: Random House, 1989). The Earthworks Group, *Fifty Simple Things You Can Do to Save the Earth*, (Berkeley, Calif.: Earthworks Press, 1989).

6. *One Earth, One Future: Our Changing Environment* (Washington, D.C.: National Academy Press, 1990). *State of the World 1990,* op. cit., pages 17–38, 79–97, 173–190. The Sierra Club, 730 Polk Street, San Francisco, CA 94109. *The End Of Nature,* op. cit. London AP dispatch, May 26, 1990. "Under the Sun—Is Our World Warming?", *National Geographic,* October 1990.

7. *State of the World 1990,* op. cit., pages 3, 62–63, 101–133. *The End of Nature,* op. cit.

8. "A Search for Water," *The Washington Spectator,*

September 15, 1989; P.O. Box 20065, London Terrace Station, New York, NY, 10011. *State of the World 1990*, op. cit., pp. 3–16, 39–58.

9. "Popline," Population Institute, 110 Maryland Avenue, NE, Suite 207, Washington, DC 20002. Zero Population Growth, 1400 16th Street, NW, Washington, DC 20036. "Saving Planet Earth," *The Washington Spectator,* January 15, 1990, op. cit. Paul Ehrlich, *The Population Bomb* (New York: Ballantine Books, 1968).

10. Center for Economic Conversion, 222C View Street, Mountain View, CA 94041. "Converting to a Peaceful Economy," *State of the World 1990,* op. cit., pp. 154–172. "Military Cuts: Disaster or Boon?" Institute of Human Relations, Loyola University, New Orleans, LA 70118. Friends Committee on National Legislation, op. cit. Peace Development Fund, 44 North Prospect Street, P.O. Box 270, Amherst, MA 01004. SANE/FREEZE, 1819 H Street, NW, Washington, DC 20006. "Swords Into Plowshares: Converting to a Peacetime Economy," Michael Renner, Worldwatch Paper 96, June 1990, 1776 Massachusetts Avenue NW, Washington, DC 20036.

11. General Accounting Office, Washington, DC 20002.

12. Catherine Drinker Bowen, *Yankee from Olympus* (Boston: Little, Brown & Co., 1944), p. 419.

13. William Stringfellow, *My People Is the Enemy: An Autobiographical Polemic* (New York: Holt, Rinehart & Winston, Anchor Books, 1966), pp. 3–4.

Chapter 12: Be Ever the Advocate

1. *The Christian Century,* 407 South Dearborn Street, Chicago, IL 60605.

2. *Christianity and Crisis,* 537 West 121st Street, New York, NY 10027.

3. *The Nation,* 72 Fifth Avenue, New York, NY 10011.

4. Foreign Policy Association, 729 Seventh Avenue, New York, NY 10019.